Can You Help Me?

Can You Help Me?

A Guide for Parents

A. H. Brafman

KARNAC

LONDON   NEW YORK

First published in 2004 by
H. Karnac (Books) Ltd.
6 Pembroke Buildings, London NW10 6RE

British Library Cataloguing in Publication Data

A C.I.P. for this book is available from the British Library

ISBN: 185575-311-1

10 9 8 7 6 5 4 3 2 1

Edited, designed, and produced by Communication Crafts

Printed in Great Britain

www.karnacbooks.com

For Miriam, with thanks
for her inspiration and support

CONTENTS

5   Guilt, honesty

6   Needing help, seeking help

It was my daughter, Miriam Speers, who conceived the idea for this book. During discussions we had about parenting, she thought I should write down my ideas so that others might benefit from them. She formulated most of the questions and encouraged me to address the challenge of answering them. I am truly grateful to her.

I thank Brett Kahr, who read the text and recommended it to Karnac. I am grateful to Oliver Rathbone, who decided to publish the book and organized further questions that were incorporated in the text. My thanks also to Eric King, who gave a proper shape to the text.

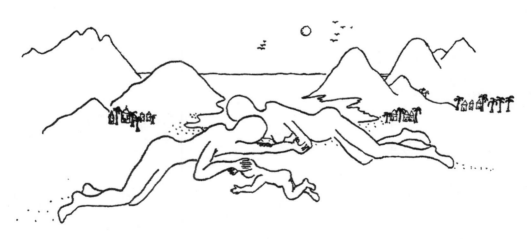

"A Safe Harbour" by Miriam Speers

Dr A. H. BRAFMAN is a psychoanalyst of adults and children. He worked with children and adolescents in the public health service (NHS) for over thirty years. This work and his training in adult and child psychoanalysis helped him to understand the psychology of individuals, but his public and private work with young people led him to recognize the importance of the actual, overt and covert interactions between parents and children. He came to realize that if children can develop pathological features as a result of their upbringing, it was equally true that, given adequate help, parents were also invaluable therapeutic agents.

Besides his private clinical practice, Dr Brafman lectures to medical students and to psychoanalytic and psychotherapy trainees, and he also acts as consultant to organizations caring for children and adolescents. He has previously published *Untying the Knot* (2001, Karnac).

There are so many books available telling parents how to bring up their children that the question arises: why another one? I want to believe that the present text offers two features that put it in a small minority of the books found in the bookshops. First, it tries to focus on situations as perceived by the child, rather than the usual observer's view of the child's behaviour. Second, it offers only a minimal number of answers. Instead, I have tried to discuss each question in such a way as to open up various possible solutions and leaving the final choice to the parents. This approach is because I have come to believe that finding an answer to a problem is much easier when one understands what relevant issues are involved. Because no two children are completely equal and the circumstances in which parents bring up each child are always changing, I think that an outsider can only give valid advice if he or she actually meets that particular set of parents and children. My intention, therefore, was to stimulate thought rather than to offer answers that, however plausible, might be of no actual relevance to the problems of the individual reader.

In my clinical work with children and parents, I have often found that parents very easily feel that they are being held responsible for their children's difficulties. Most parents already tend to blame themselves for their children's problems, but this becomes a much more painful situation if the professional appears to confirm these anxieties. I have on many occasions recognized that the phrasing of my comments had lent itself to such an interpretation, and I have then tried hard to correct this impression. My basic clinical posture is to believe very strongly that parents tend to be the best source of help for their child. Of course, there are many children who have a constitutional element that predisposes them to developmental problems, and these children need and deserve specialized professional help. But whether a problem is innate or the result of the child's interaction with the parents, their living together leads to the development of a vicious circle where the child's and the parents' words and attitudes repeatedly confirm their preconceptions. In other words, by the time child and parents come to consult the professional, they are living within a self-perpetuating vicious circle where it is virtually impossible to establish which of them, and when and how, first gave origin to that pattern of interaction. This is why I believe it to be very important to help parents to understand how they can contribute to breaking this vicious circle—that is, I see them as a precious source of help for the child.

Some of the questions in the book are answered as if addressed to the person implied in the title of that question. Others are answered as if the topic were being discussed in general terms. I hope this will not cause confusion to the reader. Another matter to be explained is my using masculine pronouns when referring to children in general, reserving "she" to those occasions when a girl is explicitly involved. Using "he or she" too often becomes intrusive, so I have only used this when clarity demanded it. Finally, in line with my psychoanalytic elders, I tend to refer to "mother" when, strictly speaking, I should use "parents". I tried to avoid confusion over this detail of style and I apologize for any lack of clarity in this respect.

A. H. Brafman

THE CHILD

Why are routines important for infants?

I remember once commenting to a paediatrician that a certain mother was not dealing properly with the crying of her very young infant. Smiling gently, he reassured me: "Don't worry, the baby will teach her . . .". What he meant was, however small and fragile they look, most infants are sturdy and quite determined to convey their needs to the world. But conveying needs is not enough: it is the parents who have to make the decisions that will ensure their infant's survival and shape him into "their child". Because they themselves are entitled to their private lives, this brings up the question of routines. At the end of the day, routines benefit both infant and parents.

It is through routines that infants acquire the learning necessary for their psychological and physical development. This development will, of course, be influenced by the individual infant's inborn emotional and physical characteristics—and here we are in the dark: only with the passage of time can we discover the infant's actual needs and abilities. We can, however, get a much clearer picture if we focus on the infant's environment, as this is under the influence of the parents and they will be able to express their own ideas about how their child should be brought up. Some parents are quite methodical, others less so, working mothers have constraints they cannot shift, and some parents devote their entire time to their children. If only all mothers and fathers gave themselves the right to have a private life, they might find their parenting "duties" easier to handle!

Caring for infants—especially for a new baby—is always a formidable challenge, but it is made no easier by the myths, advice, and recommendations that bombard parents, especially the mother. These can leave a parent feeling that certain routines are imperative, or advisable, or cruel, depending on the expert who has made the pronouncement: "Infants should be fed every three hours and refused food in the night." . . . "Never allow your baby to sleep in your bedroom." . . . "Crying babies will soon learn that it is pointless to cry, if they are just left alone." Early in the last century, a famous British doctor, Frederick Truby King, proposed a method of upbringing that was based on the assumption that babies were totally pliable: the parents were told that as long as they were sufficiently firm and determined, their infants would turn into well-tuned, organized, methodical children. A few decades later came precisely the opposite recommendation: mothers were urged to give babies the freedom to find their own rhythms: the "feeding-on-demand" notion. But as well as professionals, many mothers have their own mother (and that of their partner) in the picture. Of course, this is always a blessing, but one that has become rather rare these days because of greater mobility and migrations. At the same time, each grand-mother will have her own set of preconceptions, and some mothers may experience considerable conflict when trying to reconcile words of (sup-posed) maternal wisdom with (supposedly well-founded, scientific) profes-sional advice, not to mention their own ideas.

Focusing on the baby's needs, I follow the idea that because of the way our bodies are neurologically "wired", we have a tendency to form patterns that become self-perpetuating. I usually quote two examples to illustrate this: one is the way in which you will always wake up during the night at the precise time at which you had woken the previous night when, exception-ally, you needed to go to the toilet; another is the pattern that most people acquire of opening their bowels at the same time each day.

We know that normal babies will develop behaviour patterns that stem both from their inborn endowment—what they are born with—and from the environment to which they are exposed—the influences within and from outside the family. Perhaps it is impossible to ascertain the extent to which each of these factors determines how a particular child grows up. Babies will become hungry because their bodies require nourishment, but each baby will express this hunger in his own way. Crying is obviously taken as the typical means through which hunger is conveyed to the world. But the infant has a very limited repertoire of ways in which to express his sense of discomfort and/or need. In the scientific literature there are many arguments debating whether a baby's crying is a communication, but I prefer to see it as the expression of a physical and/or emotional state. Indeed, if someone responds to the crying, the baby may (quickly or slowly) learn what response that crying produces: here, we can speak of a communication. If, however, we focus on some early, primitive point of development, then the baby's crying has to be seen as a physiological manifestation, much as his moving his limbs has the same significance. This is relevant because there will be crying when hungry and there will be crying when there is pain, much as there will be crying when the baby cannot breathe freely.

From the parents' perspective, the picture is dramatically different. Crying immediately produces the reaction: "What does he want? What can I do to soothe him?" We will find an immensely varied display of reactions to the baby's crying. Some mothers claim that they can distinguish between crying that means hunger and crying that points to other needs the baby is trying to express. Most mothers will respond to an infant's crying by giving him the breast. If the baby won't stop crying, some mothers will try to pick him up and walk around the room, others will check the state of the nappy, and still others will experience an upsurge of anxiety. It can be disturbing for an observer to see the latter type of mother, since her anxiety tends to arouse further crying in the baby. The mother's anxiety tends to appear when she feels that her attempt to help the baby has not worked, and she experiences this as a failure on her part. Helplessness and guilt are soul-destroying emotions, and they interfere with the mother's capacity to take stock of the situation. Lucky, therefore, is the mother who takes the baby's continuing to cry after being fed as no more than an indication that he needs or wants something else.

In the matter of routines, the crucial point is the capacity to take stock and have a second look at the situation if the infant is not responding according to the parents' expectations. If, as time goes on, it becomes clear that the parents cannot find a way of coping with their infant's demands, we can only hope that they will recognize that the child's needs are not being met and, accordingly, look for help. It is extremely painful to find a parent who experiences an overwhelming sense of failure because the baby won't stop crying—in most cases, it is the infant who has a problem, not the parent. Rather than struggling against guilt and a sense of failure, it is much better to turn to a good health visitor, the family doctor, or a paediatrician.

Is it possible to "baby" a child too much?
Can affection become a hindrance?

I believe it is important first to establish *who* is evaluating a particular piece of behaviour as "babying": the child? yourself? your partner?

Let me recount two stories that might be pertinent. Many years ago I saw a lady who complained of depression and a general sense of pointlessness about life. She had four children and was happily married. We talked about her personal history and the successful way in which she had brought up her children. She was 42 years old, which at the time we were meeting was considered far from a young age for a woman. She had felt depressed at several previous times in her life, and this occasion didn't seem to point to any events that might have triggered off her feelings. However, I suddenly noticed that her four children had been born at five-year intervals, and the youngest was now nearly 5 years old. When I called her attention to this she began to cry, and we could then work out that, as each of her children started to attend primary school when they reached 5 years of age, she felt that there was no further purpose for her in life.

Some years later, I was involved in a piece of research on baby deliveries at home and in hospital. As we questioned a number of pregnant women, I found myself formulating a question that my co-workers thought was quite absurd: "When does the baby you are carrying first become a child?" We had all met women who *knew* they were pregnant but who only became convinced they were carrying a baby when they felt its first movements. But we were quite surprised at the number of different answers we received to this question! Some mothers stated very firmly that they had a baby from the moment the first period was missed, and we found some who claimed they *knew* they were carrying a new child from the morning after the significant intercourse. Yet others said that this sense of being the mother of a baby would only appear after the baby was born. Having discovered such variations, this question was put to other mothers seen in different contexts, and it became clear that many women have a precise awareness of what ages of their children they feel most comfortable with. However trivial this may appear, it can be quite amazing to observe how such sentiments can affect a woman's mothering of her children.

Most parents—perhaps *all* parents—will argue that they do not differentiate between their children, that all of them are "treated equally". This is unlikely, not in the sense of a deliberate lie, but rather because our feelings towards each of our children involve an enormous number of factors, most of which operate at an unconscious level. This is not a question of choosing which child to favour and which child to "ignore". Perhaps I should mention a few examples. A woman whose father dies not long before her delivery may name her son after her father and see the child as a new version of the loved parent she has lost. Another child born after a miscarried pregnancy may be seen as a replacement. A child born prematurely may lead the parents to develop a pattern of intense protectiveness in spite of all reassurances the doctors may give them. The same may occur when a child requires serious surgery in the early months or years of life. Quite often, if one of the parents leaves or dies, the other parent may attempt to make up for that missing parent by treating the child in ways that may be seen and/or experienced as over-protective.

In practice, most parents would be unwilling—actually, unable—to put into words what each child means to them. But it is this private meaning that explains the word "babying". Your partner may protest, quietly or loudly, and accuse you of letting your child "get away with murder", of over-protecting and babying him or her, but the chances are that in each such situation you will say that it is your partner who is being unreasonable or rigid or with too-high expectations from the child. Similarly, your child may protest that you do not let him do things that all his peers are allowed to do, and, if you believe that your child is vulnerable or in some way brittle, you are most unlikely to take your child's words as cues to judge his real abilities.

This pattern can be seen most clearly with children who develop an illness like asthma, diabetes, epilepsy, or some other kind of special sensitivity to internal or environmental agents. How can a parent be expected to "treat the child normally" when it is so difficult, if not impossible, to gauge how far to protect the child or to suspend this protection?

In other words, giving the child precisely that amount of affection that is completely age-appropriate and matches perfectly your partner's view of what is "appropriate" caring is an ideal that is virtually impossible to achieve. And you can see how infinitely more complicated this issue becomes when we (at last!) bring into the equation your child's personality. By the time you are hit by the quandary "am I babying him too much?" it is certain—whether you can recognize it or not—that you are involved in a pattern of relationships where it may be impossible to discern what is cause and what is effect. You may think the alleged "babying" is your fault, but it is an absolute certainty that someone else will tell you that it is your child who is "manipulating" you to obtain that "babying". Theoretically, there is a precise moment when the pattern was established because of particular circumstances that justified it; in practice, by the time the issue comes to be considered, those reasons have long been lost in the hazy past.

I listed above a number of rather dramatic events and circumstances that can produce heightened distress and, consequently, one or more unusual responses in the parent–child pair. But even in more ordinary, unfolding normal life we can find situations that lead to the "babying" pattern. Sometimes a row between the parents will lead to the child being allowed to sleep in the parents' bed, and this can turn into a habit. Or the child runs a high temperature, and a parent sleeps in the child's bed, leading to colossal protests from the child when the parent wants to go back to sleeping in his or her own bed. You can find a child who refuses to eat some particular food unless it is mashed; then, without any specific decision being taken, you wake up one day to find that all that child's food is being mashed before going to the table. A toilet-trained child may one day have an "accident" and, somehow, that one-off nappy may again become an obligatory piece of his clothing. Then there is the child who cannot give up his dummy, or the child who has a tummy-ache when it is time to go to nursery or school, and so on.

The impression I have formed in the course of my work is that there is a particular occasion when the child requires a special provision, something that departs from the ordinary, daily ritual that had come to be established in his life. The following day, the child may well be anxious that "the same thing" will happen again. It then seems to make all the difference in the world whether the parent feels equally anxious and decides to give the child "the benefit of the doubt" or whether, instead, the parent firmly reassures the child that his anxiety is unwarranted and demands the return to the previous habitual pattern. The explanation? I believe it is terribly simple: the parent's reaction of "giving in" convinces the child that his anxiety is fully warranted. If this sequence is repeated, the child can even come to believe that his original behaviour—which was probably a reaction to his own fear and anxiety—is, in fact, what his parent expects from him.

You may think that this explanation is too far-fetched or contrived, but I have found it to be the case time and again when dealing with phobic children. If I can be forgiven for a bit of black humour: children exclusively given organic foods to eat may well feel desperately ill if they are suddenly fed ordinary foods at a friend's house. The rationale behind this is that children do interpret the way they are treated and they behave accordingly—but they can only achieve this understanding on the basis of their capacity at each particular age.

In summary, "babying" or giving "normal" affection lies essentially in the eye of the beholder. Once you do come to formulate the present question, I suggest you ignore whoever it is who is levelling the criticism at you and try to pick up some instances of the "babying" and put these instances under the microscope. Get yourself to consider how you would treat another child under the same circumstances, and then try to remember how your parents treated you when you were in that position as a child. You—and only you— can achieve a convincing second look at the pattern and, hopefully, discover whether there is "babying" going on. If you conclude it is there, then the next challenge is to find why that "babying" ever came into being. At that point, it is worth remembering that it is a universal desire of parents that their children should "grow up" and give the parents more freedom, so "babying" would suggest that something has been taken out of proportion.

Should I let my child make mistakes— and then help pick up the pieces?

This is a rather ambiguous question. If a child "makes a mistake", "picking up the pieces" might refer to dealing with any actual injuries or to his sense of shame or guilt at doing something that brought about an unwanted consequence. But you might also be referring to "picking up the pieces" of these consequences—for example, whether the child's pocket money should be stopped to cover the costs of repairing some broken piece of furniture. Sometimes such situations are complicated by the possibility that the parent feels guilty for allowing the child to engage in an activity from which, because of his age, he should have been protected.

I would prefer to think about this question in terms of "learning from mistakes", as this somehow allows us more room for manoeuvre and yet still, I hope, meets the point of the original formulation. The crucial point in either case lies in the difference between a mistake committed by a child through ignorance and another by a child who is familiar with the correct way of doing whatever is involved. Let us consider them separately.

By definition, a child is forever learning something new. There will be many times when adults are fully convinced that the child *knew* what to do in a particular situation, whereas the child may have been misled by some unexpected detail he thought was important. The way we deal with such situations is totally dependent on how *we*, the adults, feel at the time. If in a good mood, we will give the child the benefit of the doubt, while if it happens at a point when we are already tense and frustrated, all hell breaks loose. Of course, ideally, before throwing accusations at the child, we should explore why he behaved in that "wrong" fashion: a counsel of perfection.

In this chapter of "ignorance", I have my own philosophy. Many children fail to learn a multitude of ordinary things because the parents want to protect them from harm. My favourite example is the question of plugs and sockets. In England, virtually every socket has a safety switch that has to be turned on before the socket becomes live, but this is not the case in most other countries. I believe it is important to teach every child how to deal with the electrical sockets in the house, with or without switches: knowing how to avoid danger is infinitely better than risking an accident due to ignorance. It is impossible to list all similar dangers, but, to my mind, the all-important factor in these lessons in practical, daily life lies in each parent's conception of what constitutes danger. I see no point in simply urging a parent that he should teach his child how to deal with those funny holes in the wall where the Hoover gets plugged in. If the parents embark on this lesson in an anxious frame of mind, the child is bound to sense this anxiety, and, whatever words or gestures are employed, it is the anxiety that the child will react to.

Some years ago, psychologists conducted an extremely interesting piece of research. They built a table with a thick glass top, above a patterned floor. Part-way along, the pattern stopped, and, though the floor and the glass top continued, looking from above the impression created was that of a precipice. Babies a few months old were put on this surface, while their mothers stood at the other ("precipice") end. The babies would crawl towards the mother, but as soon as they reached the end of the pattern, they would look up at her face. If the mother had a worried face, they would immediately stop and perhaps crawl backwards. But if she smiled encouragingly, they would continue to crawl forward!

I have always felt that this experiment is a wonderful example of how children learn to cope with the challenge of the unknown. This, I believe, refers to children of any age. We learn not only from words and/or gestures, but also from the emotional charge with which the lesson is conveyed. The child will always perceive and interpret new situations in line with his previous experiences, preconceptions, and abilities: the older the child, the wider the range and depth of these memory traces. And, of course, the relationship between the child and the adult concerned is a most important factor. Teaching a child how to cross a road might be an example. It is up to the adult to explain the importance of watching the traffic and waiting for a safe time to cross, but the degree of apprehension the child associates with the enterprise will depend much more on the nuances attached to the way the lesson is given. Nevertheless, no matter what an adult says or does, there will always be a child who wanders across the road blindly and another who decides to "dare" whatever dangers might exist and still another who becomes totally panic-stricken at the very thought of crossing a road.

Much more complex is the challenge of dealing with the child who makes a mistake when doing something that he normally performs without a hitch. "Why on earth did you *do* that?" . . . "What on earth got into you?" . . . "Could you really not let us have some moments of peace?" . . . "My god! Look at it!" . . . "*Wow*! That was really something!" . . . "Well, well, well . . . you were really quiet for far too long, weren't you?" . . . "And what will be *next*?" These are just a few of the expostulations that tend to erupt. As adults, we can perhaps agree that we are not made of very perfect materials and the chances of our "letting the child make mistakes" with no dramatic intervention that might possibly cause after-effects in the child is quite remote! It is very easy to preach tolerance, patience, kindness, forgiveness, and other such virtues; the trouble is that even though we all, each one of us, subscribe to this faith, the problems of daily life simply end up not allowing us to put this into practice.

I firmly believe that accidents occur and that not all our actions are dictated by unconscious feelings or wishes. The problem is that whatever accident befalls us, feelings are aroused, and by the time we stop to think about these feelings, it can be quite impossible to establish whether they preceded or were caused by that particular happening. In practice, there will always be a clever "friend" who will joke about the unconscious determinant of some accident. When dealing with a child, the typical sequence is for an adult, parent, or any relative or friend to maintain that the undesirable event demonstrates a particular (usually negative!) characteristic of the child—"Wow! You *are* clumsy!" . . . "Why are you *always* in your dream world?" . . . "You just *never* pay attention to what you're doing!" Clearly, this is not helpful, since the child may gradually come to believe that this is a true picture of his being. And this can become even more noxious when the adult takes the accident personally: "You just could not let me have a quiet morning, could you?" . . . "Oh, *no*—I've just finished cleaning the whole room!" However sincere and spontaneous such utterances can be, the child is certainly bound to feel guilty for what he has caused the parent to feel.

For better or worse, we can only *hope* to behave in some ideal way. Considering the painful fact that we cannot help being human and, therefore, fallible, the only solution is to retain a reasonable capacity for self-criticism. After all, if we catch ourselves having said to the child something that we wish we had not said, there is nothing to stop us from saying a sincere "sorry".

As for "picking up the pieces", it is important to remember that most children will blame themselves for whatever mistake they have made. However desirable it is to help the child to build or repair his self-esteem and self-confidence, this is not really an easy task. Certainly, I would strongly urge all parents not to tell a child that the "mistake" he made "does not really matter" and proceed as if it had never happened. Depending on the child's age, he is very likely to have a shrewd awareness of having done something wrong, so it is better to acknowledge the mistake and then help the child to put right whatever he has done wrong. The psychoanalytic concept that covers this is called "reparation"—this is based on the theory that the unconscious of the child experiences the "mistake" as if it had resulted from a hostile impulse towards a person, not just a "thing". It follows that the child would feel guilty and then expect that some retaliatory punishment might take place. The child's proceeding to put things right and to make up for his mistake is then experienced as a way of "repairing" whatever damage occurred to the person (in the child's unconscious). The parent acknowledging that something was wrong and offering to help the child to put it right ("pick up the pieces") may be experienced by the child as that (unconsciously attacked) person not harbouring a grudge against him—and this may assuage the sense of damage inflicted and the resulting guilt.

Going back to the start of this question: the main reason I moved away from the phrase "letting the child . . ." is because his mistakes are not really in your hands—they will occur whatever you do or fail to do. I chose, instead, "learning from the mistakes" because this helps to emphasize the crucial role that parents have in this learning process.

I'm told I should put myself in my child's shoes: what does this mean, and how do I do it?

Putting yourself in somebody else's shoes is called "empathy". The notion is clear enough: "If I put myself in your shoes, I can see that . . ." Strangely enough, though, not everyone can do this, and seeing oneself in a child's shoes would seem to be particularly difficult to achieve. "There but for the grace of God go I" expresses a similar kind of concept, but without there being any question of actually knowing or imagining how the other person feels: the focus is more on the external circumstances that have befallen someone and the conclusion that one would not like to experience that position. Perhaps I am just getting lost in the words, but I do think that this is not the same as trying to empathize with that person and figure out how exactly *he or she* is feeling. If people are asked whether they can empathize with another person ("Can you imagine how he feels?"), the answer will always be: "Yes, of course!" If then asked to describe their idea of how that person actually feels, there is a good chance that they may do no more than reveal how *they* would feel in that situation, but in a manner that the person concerned may deny has any resemblance to what *he* feels.

Empathizing is not simply a matter of will. It seems to be a personality attribute that some of us possess, but others seem to lack. In practice, most of us tend to face the world on the basis of assuming that everybody else shares our own perceptions. It takes a special endowment to be able to take on board the other person's reaction, and it is even more difficult—to complicate matters further—to wonder whether this reaction is somehow related to our contribution to the interaction.

Two brief stories to illustrate my argument: At one time, I was running a seminar on child psychoanalysis. One of the students had practised as an adult analyst for many years and was now training as a child analyst. He presented an analytic session with a child, and I was struck by a sense of flatness or deadness in his account. His comments on the child's play and utterances seemed plausible, but there was something missing in the inter-action. I decided to ask him about his previous contacts with children. He was married but had no children of his own, and it turned out that his analytic child patient was, in fact, the first child he had ever been so close to for any length of time. The "flatness" I had perceived was due to his interpreting and addressing the child with no consideration for the child's actual level of understanding and command of language.

On another occasion, I was supervising a child psychotherapist's long-term work with a child. Being experienced in this work and well informed on the literature, she could regularly give the child comments on the unconscious content of the child's play. Because of her training, she tended to emphasize what is called the "transference relationship"—that is, what the child's communications revealed of the child's feelings about her, the therapist. But we were now discussing a child with severe communication difficulties, and it became increasingly clear that the child was not responding to the therapist's interpretations. These were very formal and well-articulated pronouncements. It suddenly occurred to me that the child was trying to engage the therapist in his play, and her responding with these "professorial" comments was experienced by the child as a pushing-away manoeuvre. I finally said that she might achieve better contact with the child if she simply accepted *engaging in play* with the child, as an equal. She was quite dumbfounded. Her reaction was not due to seeing my comment as a heresy, but, rather, to her belief that "playing" is not quite the same as "treating": she felt competent with the latter, but the former seemed to her an exercise that had no place in a therapeutic setting.

I could give many other examples where adults have tried to understand a child solely on the basis of their experiences with other adults, since they had no experience of actually *playing with or coming close to* a child.

We also find many parents who are unable to empathize with their children—which is why this present question arises! To my regret, I have not discovered how to enable someone to be empathetic: it is a capacity that cannot be acquired. The best—if not the only—way of helping parents (or anyone) who become aware of this shortcoming and yet wish to make up for it is to give them the one rule they need to follow: Don't *tell* the child, *ask* the child. I will try to explain this recommendation.

I have found that people can be divided into two categories: those who are totally convinced that their assessment of a situation is the one and only possible reading there can be, and those who can accept that another person might actually experience it in some different way. In my experience, age is not relevant in this classification. It is a question of being able to conceive of another person as being a distinct, separate individual. You may be more familiar with the notion of I and you, the self and the other. This is not just a question of recognizing "the other" as somebody else, but the deeper and more subtle awareness that the other person will have his own capacities, experiences, needs that will affect his perception of what is happening.

I think that another, more complex factor is also involved in this issue: the capacity to tolerate *doubt*. The person who believes that the whole world runs in line with his own private views is well able to hold on to a certainty of knowing what belongs where. I am not speaking of someone who is deluded, but the ordinary person who assumes that everyone thinks and feels like him, until some apparently normal reaction jolts him. The classic joke of the mother who makes her son put on an overcoat because she is feeling cold illustrates this point. A more pertinent example can be found in the nursing of infants: some mothers are convinced that they *know* exactly what the child is feeling; as a result, if the child does not respond to their ministrations, they panic. This contrasts with other mothers who will move from one assumption to the next, trying to guess what the child's crying is *actually* indicating: change his nappy, wind him, give him a cuddle, feed him, and so forth.

Dealing with children who can actually put into words what they are feeling, my rule of "asking the child" comes to life. The natural impulse of virtually all parents is to comfort their children. If a child is crying, misbehaving, appearing tired or bored, showing or speaking about frightening things or people, parents will promptly try to reassure him. My advice is that *before* setting out to reassure, it is important to try to get the child to help the parents to understand what bothers him. This is not easy—in fact, it is very difficult indeed! The main stumbling block is that, more often than not, the child does not know how to articulate what he is worried, upset, angry, or frightened about. This means that parents have to be prepared to help him find his way to discovering the words that might convey what is on his mind. Repeating this in different words: rather than trying to comfort the child, the challenge is trying to help him to share with you what is upsetting him. This reformulation is important because the way in which you define your goal is bound to have an enormous influence on your approach to the task. The secret rationale for this rule is the wish to convince the child that we actually want to know how he is feeling. This is bound to help the child's self-esteem and increase his confidence in enjoying parental interest and support. From our own point of view, if the child "opens up", then the objective of "putting yourself in his shoes" is made much easier.

Another small example: when visiting a new doctor, it doesn't take too long to realize whether he intends just to give us a prescription or whether he wants to go into the details of our complaint. In practice, because we are feeling ill and anxious to get better, we are likely to ignore the doctor's idiosyncrasies and just move on. But what is it that is so special about a doctor who asks questions and actually deals with the patient's answers? This argument can be phrased in many different ways, but essentially we feel more comforted because he shows an interest in learning about our state of mind and not just our physical condition. He is dealing with us as human beings, not just as carriers of disease. If the doctor maintains this attitude, it is likely that we will report that "he cares and he understands how I feel". Perhaps it is not too scientific to say this, but human warmth and interest do appear to have a powerful therapeutic effect! I believe that a very similar process takes place when we show an interest in knowing what our child thinks and feels.

In practice, trying to get "inside the child's shoes" can be a taxing and sometimes frustrating exercise. Most of the time, we have to rely on our intuition and our underlying love and concern for the child. The danger to watch out for is that moment when patience is exhausted and we decide that "we know what he wants, anyway". Understandable, forgivable, of course—but it is still worth remembering that, in the long run, empathizing with one's child is a rewarding exercise.

I have gone on at such great length because I strongly believe that "putting oneself in one's child's shoes" is immensely important if we really wish to understand how the child is feeling; our efforts can gradually build up a gratifying response of trust, confidence, and gratitude that can be matched by very few other situations in life. I have no doubt, however, that there are thousands of parents who have no capacity for empathy yet convey to their children their love and their wish to make them happy.

How can I listen properly to my child— and hear what he is really saying?

I wish it were possible to "listen" as the result of simply following someone's advice! It is, in fact, quite a mystery why it is that some people are able to "listen" to someone else's words without any effort. We can, of course, recognize instantaneously whether we are facing a person who is able to listen or, contrariwise, whether this is someone who is definitely not interested or not able or not prepared to listen to what we might want to say. I have tried to puzzle out the reason for this curious personal characteristic, and I can only give you some tentative explanations.

Some professional people—doctors, dentists, computer technicians, gardeners—see the limit of their job as providing a solution for somebody's particular problem. This means that as soon as they feel confident they know the answer, they switch off, telling you to stop your story, or else letting you carry on even though they are no longer listening—the doctor who just aims to issue a prescription being an obvious example of this. This attitude of limited interest may, however, sometimes stem from a deliberate choice not to get involved in emotional issues. I have always admired one of my surgery teachers who told us that he did not want to get involved with the patient as a person: "I see my job as curing them of their illness, and I know that if I get emotionally involved with them, my thinking is clouded." Such a posture, resulting from insight, has to be praised. Most frequently, however, this stance of limited involvement is more an automatic one, and the professional may not even be aware of having adopted it. In fact, still on this same point, quite often people choose their careers (or medical speciality) already with the objective of sparing themselves the kind of contact they cannot cope with. Indeed, a similar posture can be found in those people who decide they do not wish to have or to look after children.

With parents, perhaps the most common reason for "not listening" arises from a viewpoint that is usually expressed in one of two different ways. The first is the idea that the parent knows best—but this is not a statement likely to be put forward as a justification, since it is kept quite unconscious. The mother who tells her child to put his coat on since it is—that is, *she* feels—so cold demonstrates this principle in operation. The second is more interesting. You might try to check this with your friends: ask them at what age they think a child begins to think, to have a mind of his own. I doubt you will get two answers pinpointing the same age! It is very common for a parent to dictate or prescribe or advise a child to *do* something, in the firm belief that the child would never think of doing it if left to his own initiative. However unlikely this may seem, that same principle is in operation: the parent believes that the child has no valid contribution to make to the issue at stake.

So how do we decide that it is relevant, useful, appropriate, important, interesting, or perhaps even good fun to ask a child what *he* thinks about something? I remember a case involving a 2½-year-old girl who refused to have a bath. For several months, day after day, her (very experienced) mother tried all kinds of manoeuvres to get her into the bath, but without success. From a drawing she did during the consultation with me, it turned out that the child had had a goldfish that had died—and she had developed the unconscious fear that the same thing might happen to her. I know that this is a child who did not have the knowledge or the language to convey her fears, but what about an older child who refuses to go to bed because there is a ghost in his room? What about the child who, from one day to the next, develops some most irritating ritual whenever leaving a room? And the child who decides not to go to school?

Once we can establish that it is better for both child and parents that the latter should want to hear what the child says, it is most important to remember that very often the child has no conscious awareness of what exactly underlies his attitude or words. A very young child may also lack the vocabulary to convey what bothers him. But the fact remains that in the present question we have *two* participants. Whether the child *can* or *cannot* express what he feels is not something the parents can affect; but parents can work on their own attitude of receptiveness, interest, or curiosity that will convey to the child that they care.

Perhaps it is worth adding a "rule of thumb": if you ask the child a question, you should not correct him, however he phrases his answer; instead, you should ask for an explanation or a clarification. Any "putting the record straight" will be experienced by the child as a statement of what you want to hear—and few children will question this.

How important is "quality time"? How do I foster intimacy without making my child "sit and talk"?

Providing quality time while a child is growing up is important—very important. But, sadly, this cannot be done on prescription. Some parents enjoy lying on the carpet or on the bed, reading stories to their toddler; others enjoy taking their child to the park or the swimming-pool—the variations are endless. I remember a father taking his son for bicycle rides, with the child sitting behind him wearing the prescribed helmet: I thought this was an unusual expression of togetherness, wondering what the child got out of watching his father's back. But who knows? Perhaps the son did enjoy exploring the streets in that way. The point here is that each parent must discover something he or she enjoys and the child enjoys too. It is probably useless to engage in "quality time" when all one feels is the wish to try to "do the right thing by the child".

I believe quality time must never be adopted *as a means* of achieving closer intimacy. However unrealistic it may sound, to me "quality time" implies spontaneity and pleasure. Perhaps I could be excused for a story that might appear too remote and unrelated. I worked for several years in a psychiatric hospital where drugs were not used and patients were treated only with psychotherapy, both singly and in groups. Every morning all patients and all nurses, together with some of the doctors, held a "community meeting", at which all kinds of problems were discussed; similarly, mid-morning all doctors and nurses had a 20-minute coffee break, where they met to chat and simply spend some time together. At one point, I commented on how pleasant these meetings were, but I also wondered about the ritualistic element involved—absentees were ticked off! The explanation: one of the pioneers of psychoanalysis in Britain, John Rickman, was a Quaker. When the Second World War broke out and wounded soldiers needed psychiatric hospitalization and help to recover from war traumas, Rickman was one of the consultants in charge of the main centre for their rehabilitation (Northfield Hospital). He introduced, as part of hospital life, morning community meetings, where all the patients, nurses, and doctors met to discuss the problems of living and working together. I learnt that these morning meetings, where thoughts and feelings are voiced and shared with all others, are an integral part of Quaker philosophy. As time went on, many other hospitals began to offer "community treatment", and the same principle has been adopted elsewhere; for example, by A. S. Neill at his Summerhill School. When all participants are seen as sharing the same community, hierarchies are preserved on the basis of respect rather than power, and a sense of equality of rights can boost the self-confidence of those who need help.

I think that such meetings can be considered "quality time". After we brought our family to London, we had to learn how to adapt to a new lifestyle. There was no extended family, no full-time help around the house. But, more important, both my wife and I spent most hours of the day working and studying, which meant that our older children had to learn to look after themselves, with little help from us. Somehow, evening meals became our "quality time", the point in the day when every member of the family was expected to sit down and chat and laugh and argue and find compromises. As time went by, we had innumerable guests whom we, the parents, or the children brought to the house, and more than once we heard these guests voicing their view that only a deep sense of closeness could allow for so much passion to be expressed among family members without any sign of malice or rancour.

But this is the easy part of the question—"fostering intimacy" is far more elusive. My head spins with words such as love, trust, closeness, friendship, respect, equality, seniority, dependence, and then you have the modern "boundaries" notion—terribly complex! To my mind, the biggest stumbling block is that we can only gauge, analyse, establish what *we* feel when we are interacting with another person. How this other person actually experiences our approach is totally out of our hands. Whether we consider interactions between spouses, parent and child, or any other type of encounter, it is unavoidable that each party will make conscious and unconscious assumptions as to how the other is going to react to each input. This can be seen in the classical "I know you are going to object to this, but . . ." invariably uttered in a tone of voice indicating total conviction that this warning would guarantee a different reaction! When these pairings exist in a long-term relationship, then patterns are established that become very resistant to any change.

When do the bonds of intimacy between parents and child begin to be built? Presumably, by the time we can make the child "sit and talk", these bonds have long been established (assuming we have cared for the child from birth!). If they are still not built, something must have gone wrong somewhere along the way.

A penny has dropped here: perhaps I have misunderstood your question? Or is it that you are using misleading words? I assume that "fostering intimacy" refers to a relationship of closeness, a type of togetherness that does not require explicit words to make either party feel understood by the other. This is why I mentioned love, trust, and respect. I can add "mutual understanding" and so many other features, but the point of such intimate relationships is that, however much the two parties and even any number of outsiders can recognize their presence, it may be virtually impossible to define how they came into being. They tend to be taken for granted, as something precious and valued by both parties, but something discovered rather than something they set out to achieve. Presumably, this is not the case when two adults first fall in love with each other: they will speak of giving themselves time to know each other better. But certainly with children the strength of this bond does not seem to result from a deliberate effort of either party.

I wonder whether that "making your child sit and talk" should be interpreted as a version of "playing together". There are many parents who have enormous difficulty in coping with a child's need to spend "forever" playing with toys or games. It can be extremely puzzling to understand whether the child is being deliberately off-putting, testing the parents' patience, or simply carrying on as if alone, leaving it to the parent to decide whether to stay or to leave. Very often it is not the child who has to be made to sit and talk; it is, rather, the parent who has to make this effort. As I argued above, this belongs in the realm of "quality time", and it is up to the adult to coax the child to engage in it or, at other times, to pick up whatever cue the child gives trying to engage the parent. But rightly or wrongly, I would not necessarily link the building of bonds of intimacy with playing or with quality time. This qualification is linked to that word *"building"*, which suggests effort, a deliberate move to achieve a goal. If we turned the question around and asked how bonds of intimacy come into existence, I would certainly emphasize closeness, shared activities, and mutually engaging and satisfying time together—and this would, of course, include quality time as much as it would include playing together. However, the emphasis would rest on spontaneity and pleasure, not on a sense of fulfilling a prescribed duty.

When does "making allowances" become "spoiling" or "inappropriate"?

Has there ever been a child who says that he is spoiled? Has a parent ever been found who spontaneously and sincerely admits that he or she spoils his or her child? I have never come across such people—it is always a third party who proclaims that spoiling and/or inappropriate management is taking place. The few exceptions I have found when a parent confessed to spoiling his or her child were always followed by complex justifications that emphasized that particular needs of the child compelled the parent to behave in that manner.

If you object to something your child says or does, do you consider how you will react, or do you find yourself having reacted anyway? "Making allowances" already implies that we have had time to ponder over what to do and decided not to take the child to task. Life being what it is, most of the time we find that "thinking" comes after we have already said and/or done something in response to our child's behaviour. Nevertheless, "thinking" in this case means weighing up the pros and cons of each of the many alternative ways of reacting that come to our mind. It is always difficult to decide whether our opposition results from our own needs and beliefs or, instead, from considering the child's needs and abilities. In practice, it is virtually impossible to disentangle these two: does it matter? It is worth remembering that the child, being on the receiving end of our reaction, cannot know the reasons that led us to act the way we did: whether at the point of our immediate, impulsive reaction or subsequently, when we have decided to "have a word about it". Either way and whatever our motivation, for the child our attitudes signify a statement of what we expect from him, only one more of the thousands of injunctions that shape the ethos of the family in which he is growing up.

I believe very strongly that children need clarity and consistency from their parents. If we wish to provide our child with this image of firm expectations and predictable reactions, then we must strive to achieve a clear definition of what we want our child to learn from us. As soon as we are not quite sure where we stand over any particular issue, we are in trouble. It is precisely this state of uncertainty that gives rise to the whole dilemma of making allowances, indulging, spoiling, and so forth, or, conversely, of punishing unfairly.

Complications arise when, for example, you feel guilty over some impulsive reaction. Guilt tends to cloud judgement: a good rule of thumb, if you find yourself feeling embarrassed and/or guilty about your behaviour, is that it is best to postpone action and, instead, give yourself time to think further. Disagreement between the spouses is another typical complication.

Looking at the behaviour of a particular child, one of the most difficult challenges is identifying what stems from the child's constitutional make-up and what is the result of the influences that child has been exposed to. All of us will argue that the child's temperament is inborn, but time and again we will throw in some critical observation regarding the way in which his parents brought him up. From a practical point of view, it is best to believe that the parents *can* and *do* influence the development of their child. Even if it is impossible to establish to what extent and in what manner they do it, I still think this is the best working hypothesis to adopt. Why? Because this allows parents to believe that they can contribute to the child's development and, therefore, persist in their attempt to get their views across to the child. Of course, each child has his own range of abilities and nobody can perform magic, but there is nothing more soul-destroying than the feeling that "there is nothing I can do for my child". However, if the child in question has any type of physical or psychological impediment, the parents require expert help to understand the extent to which they can, realistically, help their child.

Whatever else it means, "making allowances" describes a response to a child failing to comply with some expectation of his parents—for example, when parents decide that the child is old enough to use a knife and fork at the table, but the child fails to comply. There are so many factors that influence this apparently simple piece of behaviour that we might find it really difficult to decide whether the child is still incapable of handling the knife and fork (not ready for it) or is defying his parents (capable, but rebellious). To take another example: should the child call his parents "Dad" and "Mum", or should he use their names? With many other languages, there is a similar issue over whether the child should address the parents informally or formally, such as "*tu*" or "*vous*" in French. Decisions of this kind demand clarity and conviction, since any "making allowances" will only lead to confusion for the child—perhaps also for the parents! However silly these examples may sound, I believe they are representative of many other, more dramatic examples we might put forward. A boy hits his younger sister: if the parents decide to "give him the benefit of the doubt" because the daughter is known to drive everyone crazy with her annoying whining, this might lay the ground for serious trouble. This example shows two behaviours all parents wish could be eliminated: whining and the use of physical force. Each of these highlights a child's style of expressing his or her feelings and then the impact this has on those the child lives with. It is easy to see how the parents' intervention may be interpreted as "taking sides", but this would be losing sight of the more important issue of teaching children what is acceptable and what oversteps the line that characterizes the family ethos. A child, of course, deserves respect for his individuality, his private manner of expressing his distress or his anxiety, but from very early on he has to be made aware of the impact of his communications on those around him. There is serious danger in confusing respect for individual freedom with licence to annoy, hurt, or offend others. It is a question not of "squashing" the child's personality, but, rather, of equipping him to live in society.

One important caveat: we must never forget the possibility that we are not correctly gauging the child's ability to respond to our expectations. Age is an important factor, as is the fact that different children mature at different rates. Toilet training is the best example of this problem. No child can "obey" commands to pee into the potty if his bladder sphincters have not matured sufficiently. It becomes a complex art to gauge whether one particular incident of wetting himself is due to insufficient maturation to enable self-control or is, instead, an instance of defiance. It is very rare to find a child who wets himself as simply an act of defiance. So many factors come into play that it is best to interpret the occasional wetting as a sign that some unknown (to us!) anxiety has overruled the child's capacity to control his sphincters. I believe that this is the most likely interpretation in the majority of cases, because I think that, however annoyed we may become, the child's sense of pride and self-esteem is far more affected by the wetting than we may be able or prepared to recognize.

The debate over physical punishment of children is a recurring theme in our society. There is great demand for legislation to control it, but this goes beyond the scope of our discussion. The point I want to emphasize is that I believe "hitting" is not a universal piece of behaviour. We can find long and erudite arguments about the role of aggression in human endowment, but I would certainly not see "aggression" and "hitting" as synonymous. There are marked, important differences between aggression, hostility, and violence, but perhaps it is not necessary to go into these in our present context. Because "aggression" is intimately linked to self-defence, self-assertion, and self-confidence, it becomes an integral part of daily living. Nevertheless, even if no one—child or adult—can avoid experiencing aggressive impulses, we must teach our children what the acceptable ways are of expressing that aggression. And this is one of the very fascinating aspects of family life. Each family develops its own language of aggressive behaviour. In some families, hitting is used in much the same way as sarcasm is employed in other homes. Some parents punish a child by putting him to bed, others make him go without a meal. Does this make a difference? I believe it does, since the child soon learns the family's way of expressing frustration, anger, resentment, and the like. There is absolutely no way that we can face life without experiencing these emotions, and what each of us has to teach our children is what we consider a legitimate way of dealing with these feelings and what we cannot condone. And here is the vital catch: parents may want to teach this lesson through what they say, but the child only learns from the example the parents set through how they treat their child(ren) and each other.

I may appear to have drifted too far from the question, but I do think that these factors have to be taken into account before deciding when "making allowances" becomes "spoiling" or "inappropriate upbringing". Right from birth, the child learns *his parents'* language—not just the language they speak, but the thousands of small details that constitute living in that individual unit, as a family, in its society, its neighbourhood, its country. This is why each of us has to decide what we find acceptable and what behaviours we wish to stop our child from adopting. While you believe you are making allowances, somebody else may say you are spoiling your child or letting him behave inappropriately. I would suggest leaving these labels aside and, instead, consider that from the child's point of view, in all probability, there is only clarity or confusion. Whichever way your child behaves, your reaction will bring home to him where he stands in your eyes, and this is what leads the child to understand what is expected from him.

To repeat the point: I strongly believe that what is sauce for the goose is sauce for the gander. Once we allow ourselves to think that a particular behaviour is fine when practised by us but to be condemned when put into practice by our child, we are in trouble. If I voice at table my profound dislike for my mother-in-law, I must be prepared for that awful day when my child addresses granny in a voice full of hostility or contempt. If I use swear-words when addressing any member of my family, it is very likely that my children will also adopt them. Of course, children will gradually learn the importance of context, and a normal child can quickly learn the constraints imposed by the different environments in which he lives. Nevertheless, it is up to us to teach our child how he, as our child, is expected to treat other human beings. To achieve this, the first and most important example comes to be the way in which we treat him.

How can I discipline my child without using physical punishment?

The topic of discipline came up in the previous question. Each family has its own ethos. Most features are virtually imperceptible, but they are still there, influencing every member of the family. As people live together, they learn how each of the others tends to behave, and this influences the way in which they will address that person. An outsider might pick out a particular interaction and choose to define who initiated it and who responded to it—and it would never surprise me to hear the participants correcting the visitor as to who, in fact, was responsible for triggering off the clash.

I remember seeing in a child guidance clinic a 7-year-old boy with his mother, who had a history of serious mental illness. The mother's social worker was also in the room. The boy was drawing, and I was talking to the mother. She was telling me about various problems she had to face, but she was reasonably calm and collected, speaking with some confidence about her capacity to cope with life and, particularly, to look after her children. When the boy had finished his drawing, I asked him to tell me what he had drawn. I forget what exactly he said about the picture, but suddenly the mother took offence at a comment of his. She jumped out of her chair ranting and raving, saying the boy was showing her up and that she would not tolerate this—she would beat hell out of him, she would strangle him, she would teach him how to respect her, and so on. I was shocked. My words of reassurance had no effect, and the social worker's attempts to pacify the mother made no difference either. I said to the social worker that it was clearly not safe to leave the child in his mother's care. Very gently, almost tenderly, she told me that I should allow her to deal with the situation.

I left the room and went to the clinic's office. Several of my colleagues were there. They had heard the screams and were waiting to see what was going to happen. One of them, however, smiled broadly and asked me whether I had noticed the family's name. I quoted it to her and said, "So what?" "But—they are Mediterranean!" I repeated my "So what?" "Surely you must know that the mother doesn't mean a word of what she says—she is expressing her outrage in the same language in which she was brought up . . . and the son knows it, so don't worry." What could I say? I had seen pathology and danger where only "Mediterranean passion" existed. Not long afterwards, the social worker came to the office to tell me that she would take the mother and son to their house and sort the crisis out. She was quite convinced that I had overreacted and that, in the long term, all was reasonably well under control.

Parents have asked me whether or not they should hit their child. My answer has always surprised them: "It depends on how you feel about doing it." I learnt my lesson when I had parents complaining that "no matter what they said or did" to their child, it never worked—the child just carried on, ignoring their words. As parental complaints go, this is most convincing, quite beyond any questioning. But one day this scene happened in front of me during a consultation, and the penny dropped: the mother's words were meant to convey a prohibition, a condemnation, an injunction to be obeyed, if not a threat as well. But the tone of her voice very clearly signified a plea, a painful appeal that the child should not hurt her so badly. At this point, it becomes vitally important to assess whether the child's intellectual and emotional make-up are normal, whether the child is able—has the potential—to behave differently. If this is the case, my interpretation of this interaction is that as soon as the child hears the mother's voice, he registers that she feels hurt. He feels guilty for hurting her, but equally important (or more so!) is that the child feels scared that the mother is now weak, helpless, and, therefore, unable to look after him. As soon as this type of insecurity appears on the scene, the child is (unconsciously) compelled to test out the mother in the hope that she regains control and reassures him that he cannot, in fact, destroy her. Tragically, this impulse of the child's tends to reinforce the mother's view of him as "impossible" and leads to a painful vicious circle, with child and mother confirming each other's anxieties.

Perhaps my point about "hitting the child" is now clearer. Hitting or not hitting a child tends to be a redundant kind of question. On the whole, parents who feel comfortable with hitting the child will do it anyway, and those who cannot cope with it are not likely to implement it just because they are told it is acceptable or useful to do it. Those parents who oppose physical punishment (and I am one of them) will justify it in many different ways, just as those who believe in its efficacy will also put forward no end of arguments. I believe that the crucial factor to be established is the manner in which the physical punishment is embarked upon. Of course, this will tell us nothing about the way in which the child experiences it, but at least we can assess what moves the adult to do this.

But I am getting lost in "physical punishment" when the question was about "disciplining". I might perhaps recount a lesson I learnt when my daughter was in her mid-teens. I was then working with adolescents in an inpatient hospital setting, and I saw myself as something of an expert in their problems. One day, as a family we were discussing over dinner the whole question of teaching, disciplining, and the extent to which parents could concentrate on issues and put their emotions aside. I firmly believed in my capacity to be insightful and dispassionate, perhaps even objective in dealing with my children and our occasional (?) clashes. My daughter asked me, as gently as she could, whether I really believed that my eyes did not give away how I truly felt about any matter under discussion. (I thought of getting dark-tinted lenses for my glasses, but I realized I had left it too late . . .)

Another personal story, this time involving my youngest son: one evening, when he was about 4 or 5 years old, we had guests in the house. It was getting late, and I said that he should go to bed. He wanted to stay with the company, so I repeated my request, which eventually turned into a command. This performance became rather exasperating, and I ended up losing my temper. My voice was raised, and I bombarded him with questions and complaints about his stubbornness. He finally began to climb the stairs towards his bedroom, but at one point he began to cry and said to me, "You are treating me like some kind of criminal!" Some psychoanalysts would probably argue that his guilt and shame for having defied me had led him to project onto me the image of the enforcer that might punish him accordingly. This may well have been the case, but my interpretation was that his knowledge of his father (me) had led him to believe that that degree of passion was something I might display only if and when faced with someone truly dangerous.

My point is that each family develops its own style of living and, at the same time, its characteristic "language of disciplining". How can we explain that many cultures teach children to hold the fork in the left hand and the knife in the right, while other cultures do the opposite and in yet others people eat with their fingers? I always addressed my parents using the third person singular, while many of my friends would only use the second person, and others simply used their parents' names. And what of the English dictum (though now out of fashion) that "children are to be seen, but not heard"? These are examples of issues that are part of the pattern of daily life, and they are conveyed, imposed, and demanded in the individual style that characterizes each family's way of disciplining. They are meant to educate each child to be a true member of that family in which he grows up. "You live in my house, therefore you will follow my rules, my/our way of living" would be the basic philosophy of disciplining.

The situation becomes infinitely more complex when we remember that we live in a wider society and parents must enable their children to live in the community of which *all* of them are part. In the present multicultural Britain this is a topical problem, as many minority families and especially but not exclusively immigrant families try hard to preserve their original cultural inheritance. The role of the woman in the family and in society—how she dresses, what and how she studies and/or works, how she chooses a partner—are well-known fertile areas for problems in this respect. The rights and duties of the *pater familias* can also become very relevant if an adolescent child chooses to rebel and claim rights for him/herself. These are only some of the areas where the family's idea of discipline can clash with the outside society's view of life.

As long as these problems are contained within the family, society remains ignorant of their existence; but from time to time they spill out, and it can be painfully difficult to find a solution that satisfies both the family and society.

I have been consulted many times about children who present problems at school and are then taken into some form of counselling or therapy. The vast majority of therapists I have met will try to work with the child as *an individual*—that is, as if it did not matter about the child's colour, the country of origin of the parents, the religion they practised, their social class, or the structure of the family. These are all factors that have shaped that child to become the child they are seeing. To believe that a child's individuality is being respected by ignoring these cultural factors is a fiction, a serious mistake that totally bypasses the reality of the child's life.

A rather painful, new example of what I believe can be seen as part of the "disciplining" issue exploded recently in Britain: that of children who are obese because of their diet. A 12-year-old has been found who weighs 20 stone (280 pounds). A new organization has been founded to give such children a whole range of therapeutic inputs. Half a page of a newspaper was devoted to the problem, and that article mentioned—totally in passing, as if completely irrelevant—that *both* parents are grossly obese.

In summary, it is only the parents who can discipline their child—and they, for better or for worse, can only be true to their selves. There are parents who can learn and change, others who cannot. In the consulting-room, I have learnt to recognize those who belong to each category, but this is because parents will only come to consult me if they have any trace of recognition of something in themselves that needs changing. It does some-times happen that they come to me because a teacher, social worker, or lawyer has demanded a professional opinion, but it does not take long for them to reveal whether or not they believe that anything in themselves needs changing. A rather touching group of parents does exist who are aware of their limitations but still urge us or allow us to help their child, as seen by their preparedness to accept appointments for the child. I have come to refer to them as displaying a "Miriam's syndrome", a reference to Moses' sister, who ensured the boy obtained the upbringing his parents could not give him.

What does physical punishment mean to the child?

There is a wonderful Brazilian saying, "*É de pequenino que se torce o pepino*" [if you wish to shape a cucumber, you have to start from the moment it begins to grow]. How early does a child begin to learn? It is safe to assume that it starts from birth. Why will an English child learn to say "Mum" and "Dada", while a French baby is likely to say "Maman" and "Papa"? I believe the same happens about hitting. There must be a difference between hitting as a form of disciplining and hitting as an expression of sadism and abuse, but I imagine the child will only discover the difference between the two at a much later stage of his development.

It is true to say that hitting a child is a cultural issue, but I am sharpening the focus to say that it is part of a family's style—a language, as I like to call it. For the adult (and the child!), hitting is an expression of certain feelings and impulses. I assume that the same feelings will lead another person to reach for some other manner of expressing emotions, such as swearing, sermonizing, counting to ten, or saying a prayer. It is not necessarily a question of different feelings that lead to various ways of expressing them, but each individual's style of giving expression to those feelings. If A insults B, B may retaliate by voicing a similar insult, much as he may crumple up in tears or voice a sarcastic remark or punch A. For an outsider, the stimulus given by A may or may not justify B's reaction, but the two fundamental points involved in this exchange are, first, B's interpretation of A's remark and, second, B's individual style of responding to it. Obviously, the relationship between A and B is important. Nevertheless, whatever their relationship, B's response will still depend on his interpretation of A's remark, his private repertoire of self-defence reactions, and his capacity at that precise moment to scrutinize his urges and utilize his self-control to choose how he actually reacts. If self-control breaks down and B's reaction is immediate and totally impulsive, we find the classical argument as to whether his reaction was completely out of character, alien to his genuine, real self, or, alternatively, whether it had always been there, to be released the moment some threshold was crossed.

If we now see A as a parent and B as a child, how do we interpret B's reaction when he is hit by his parent, A? If it were possible to have a scientific study of this interaction, we might learn valuable lessons about the development of individual characteristics in the growing child. In ordinary life, by the time a child is brought under the scrutiny of any outsider (nursery teacher, child-minder, doctor, social worker), behaviour patterns have long been established. This can make it virtually impossible to establish whether the child's propensity to hit others reflects his constitutional endowment or is a reflection of the way he was brought up by his parents.

What does the baby/child make of being hit? I suspect that at very early stages the baby will not distinguish between being hit, being handled roughly, or being shouted at. Sometimes the baby may not even react to the intrusion; at other times he may burst out crying most plaintively. If the latter, how can we decide whether the baby has felt pain and is now experiencing fear or, instead, has been disturbed in his state of rest and is demonstrating his distress, his loss of emotional and physical equilibrium? It is very easy and tempting to imagine that the baby is feeling exactly the same as an adult would feel in that situation, but this does not make it a fact.

As the baby grows older, these stimuli will become differentiated, and we do not really know for sure how the baby comes to interpret each painful physical experience that befalls him. Once the child can put his thoughts and feelings into words, it is easier to grasp what he makes of being hit or shouted at. I am not considering the precise motivation for the parent's use of physical force, but on the whole parents will justify their use of physical punishment by claiming this to be a disciplining tool. Consequently, these parents will try very hard to make the child learn that he is not being hit gratuitously but, rather, punished for something he has done and which he must not repeat.

The parent who one day loses control and beats the child in a manner that can slip into a murderous attack probably belongs to a special, exceptional category. In this case, the age of the child is irrelevant, and we can only assume that the child will move from surprise to fear, to panic and terror. I am, instead, concentrating on the kind of "hitting" where the parent explains it as being a perfectly ordinary and justifiable attempt to teach the child how to behave. This is what leads the child to interpret the parent's behaviour and words as being triggered off by some action of his own. This is probably the reason why we find that the older child will usually blame himself for being hit. It is not difficult for an outsider to recognize that any child finds it almost impossible to label his parent as "wrong", let alone "cruel". I learnt of a different reason for this from an older child, whom I saw in therapy: "As long as I blame myself," he said, "I can hope that I will be able to prevent it from happening again."

However, at an unconscious level, beyond this issue of "who is to blame", the child learns that when hurt, annoyed, displeased, or incommoded by someone's behaviour, hitting is a legitimate way of expressing these feelings. This can already be seen in some toddlers who keep hitting their siblings: significantly, some parents will put an immediate curb on such displays of what they consider "unacceptable violence", while those parents who do hit their children will condone this manner of expressing feelings of hostility.

But not all children brought up by parents who hit them will move on to adopt this way of expressing their feelings. Some of these children will, in fact, prove totally incapable of resorting to physical violence, and this points to a capacity to assess impulses and make considered decisions about how to relate to the world around them.

From the perspective of "who is to blame?" a point is reached when the child can discern that "hitting" seems not to be related to the seriousness of the apparent offence but is, rather, a stereotypical response on the part of one or both parents. This usually signals a major upheaval, when the child experiences an intense feeling of being treated unfairly, and strong feelings of resentment come to the surface. He *knows* the parent is wrong, but how is he to deal with his new understanding? How should he protect himself? Stay silent? Run away? Cry? Wet himself? Hold his breath? Faint? Appeal to the other parent? Some children decide to bide their time and wait until that point when their physical size enables them to hit back at the parent.

Unfortunately, the majority of children find it impossible to discuss these issues with any person outside the family. Another complicating factor is the fact that, in the vast majority of families, this "hitting" goes on with the full knowledge of the other spouse, who may, sadly, also be coming in for the same kind of hitting or even using the same technique against the child. There is no doubt that the child has quite a different experience if one of the parents is able to intervene and stop the hitting, but it is difficult to predict how this will influence the child's adopting or rejecting violence as a behaviour of his own.

This change from victim to perpetrator is described by two interesting psychoanalytic concepts that are, in fact, self-explanatory: "identification with the aggressor" and "turning passive into active". For an outsider, it is immensely baffling that someone who has experienced the pain, humiliation, and, at times, helpless rage of being hit by someone in a position of authority should proceed to subject another human being to precisely the same painful experiences. For the record, I should mention that the word "sadism" is used when this violent behaviour involves the attacker deriving pleasure from the other person's pain.

Another point that arouses complex debate is whether the violent child (or adult!) brings that violence as part of his genetic endowment or whether he learns it from his environment as he grows up. Seeing an individual child who attacks a younger sibling or other children with whom he plays, it can be an enormous challenge to isolate the "real" origin of his behaviour. For me as a clinician having seen a large number of children, it has been impossible to avoid building up a number of assumptions about "violent children". The challenge lies in comparing the individual child or adult in front of me with all these assumptions. I confess that my initial assumption is that a violent child has been on the receiving end of similar violence—not because of my analytic theories, but because I see "hitting" as a language, a means of expressing strong emotions of hostility, and, like other things they learn from their parents, children who are hit are likely to learn to hit when struggling with those strong antagonistic feelings towards another person.

Is it better to send children to nursery school or to look after them at home?

Psychologists have investigated the effect of various types of nursery education on the development of children's intellectual abilities. Predictably, their statistics show that the various methods adopted by different schools have a definite influence on the achievements of the children. However, if you decide to act on these findings, how can you be sure that your child will be among those who benefited from this input or, instead, among those who failed to show that progress? But far more importantly, to the best of my knowledge all these investigations have shown that by the age of 5 or 6 years, it was no longer possible to distinguish the nursery-school children from those who had not been given this experience. So does it mean that it is pointless or counterproductive to send children to nursery school?

It is important to take into account that before they are 5 years old, many children receive formal education because of beliefs their parents hold. Parents in several religions send their children to religious educational classes from a very early age, as do parents belonging to quasi-religious or non-religious kinds of sects who send their children to classes to learn about the principles held by that particular group. Perhaps we might dismiss such classes as indoctrination and not education, but I believe they still have to be considered in terms of the present question.

In the United Kingdom children start their formal education at 5 years of age, but this starting age varies considerably in different countries; similarly, the length of the school day will vary from country to country. Nevertheless, no matter what the country, the age for university entrance is always at around 18 or 19 years—and I suspect it would be virtually impossible to guess the educational input each child has had in his earliest years. Of course, this is true only as a generalization, since they would have covered very different subjects, but on the basis of the ordinary university entrance exams, I would expect all these youngsters to perform with approximately equal chances of success.

Coming back to the question, I think that the most important point to consider is whether the choice of kindergarten, nursery school, playgroup, or regular classes, under whatever name, responds to a need of the children or to one of the parents. Take, for example, the type of story we hear from time to time about parents who dismiss the local educational services as no good, and they decide that they want their child to be taught at home, or a less rare situation in our day and age, a child with chronic fatigue syndrome (or something similar), who is kept at home, being taught by the parents—how will this affect the child's educational achievements? In what way is the child's progress influenced by these circumstances, which are totally outside the child's control?

At the time of writing these lines, heated arguments abound throughout the country regarding further subsidies for the provision of educational facilities for children under school age. What is different now is that this step is not being disguised as a new attempt to foster children's educational potentials. For a change, there is the honest admission that such facilities are needed because of the large number of families where both parents have to go out and work in full-time jobs. Sadly, this decision was taken not out of a genuine wish to help parents and children, but as a means of combating the series of scandals of children who experienced serious traumas at the hands of incompetent and/or malicious caretakers. It is a very painful development that nowadays we have so many working single parents and families where both parents work full-time. To make this problem worse, the vast majority of these parents, especially those living in London and other large cities, have no access to a supportive family network. This means that during work hours younger children have to remain with caretakers, either in a family house or in a special environment.

At the same time, there are many parents who believe that their under-5s will benefit from spending some time with other children in a supervised environment. We have to admit the impossibility of establishing the precise reason why children of working parents are placed in a nursery group or a similar facility. Before taking my argument further, I want to make quite explicit that at this time, with the profusion of competent nurseries, there is no real, objective reason for a working parent to feel shame or guilt about leaving his or her child with a reliable nursery or caretaker. Of course, it is important to obtain careful references for such an establishment or person before entrusting a child to them, but there is no reason why such a placement will, of itself, cause any damage to the child. However, feelings of shame and/or guilt can easily arise from an awareness of rules and customs that prevailed in the family of origin of that particular parent or from some critical remark made by a relative or friend. I am always bemused by people who, having voiced strong criticism of parents who leave their under-5s in a nursery for a few hours ("children need to spend time with their parents!"), send their 7-year-old to a distant boarding-school.

Having argued that very often children will be placed in a nursery school because of the parents' commitments and needs, we should turn to the children's side of the story. A nursery, playgroup, or similar establishment will make it possible for the child to take a momentous step forward in his process of socialization. If the child grows up in a small community, urban or rural, within a family network, or among neighbours who maintain a close relationship, then he has many opportunities of meeting and playing with children of similar ages. In addition to mother, there is a chance that aunts, neighbours, and older adults will give the child that special sense of protection and security that he needs when exploring the world outside the four walls of his home. We might say that the walls of the home are opened up to constitute a protective net where friendly figures help the child to discover that, apart from parents and siblings, there is also a wider world, one in which children and adults display behaviours that complement those to which the child was first exposed. But what if the child lives in a big city, or his parents have moved to a new community? No relatives, no friends, new neighbours . . . Perhaps the family are not in an openly hostile community, but it is most unlikely that at first the parents will feel comfortable about allowing their child to mingle with the other children or adults in their new neighbourhood. In such circumstances, the organized and supervised environment of a nursery school becomes a blessing for the growing child.

Unfortunately, having decided to send their child to a nursery school, most people then find that there are not so many schools to choose from. Personal recommendation from other parents counts for a lot, but I believe the most important factor to establish is the trustworthiness and reliability of the person in charge of the nursery. You want a warm adult who loves children. Even a brief conversation should allow you to decide how the person in charge sees her role vis-à-vis the children. One will tell you about the importance of teaching the child to be disciplined and responsible, much as another will tell you of the fun that can be found in spending time with a child. (I would choose the latter, but you might prefer to have the former!) What is at stake is the basic view of what a young child needs at that point of his life: the fundamentals of discipline and the groundwork for later formal learning or, alternatively, a happy atmosphere, where he learns what it means to share time with peers and caring adults. Personally, I believe the latter is a better investment for further development. Discovering how he affects strangers and how these new people treat him gives the child a unique opportunity to sharpen his awareness of himself in the world. When the child is able to trust his self-control and also learn to win friends rather than foster conflicts, he will have acquired a valuable baseline upon which to build later formal knowledge.

2 Trying their wings

How can I help my child towards becoming independent?

Nurturing is the quintessential element of that phase of the child's development that we call "dependence". Independence is the final, optimal stage in the line of growth and progress that begins with birth, when the baby is in a state of total dependence on the mother. Donald W. Winnicott, an eminent paediatrician, psychoanalyst, and child psychiatrist, wrote extensively about a baby's first months of life. He emphasized the absolutely vital importance of a nurturing mother, one who can help her baby to survive—not least because he would simply die if he had no one nurturing him—and, stage by stage, take him to that point where he is able, physically and emotionally, to survive on his own. Words such as "nurturing", "dependence", and "independence" can be used with meanings that extend from the literal to the metaphorical, but in our present context what matters at the early stages of the baby's life is the bond between mother and child and the extent to which they need each other. There is no doubt that a father is part of this picture, and we could discuss at length the precise role he plays vis-à-vis the mother and the baby. But it will be more practical to focus on "dependence" in terms of the mother–baby relationship.

Whenever we speak of a "relationship of dependence", we must define what precisely this means for each party. Colloquially, we say that the baby needs the mother, but it is equally true that the mother also needs the baby. It is, though, difficult to define the precise features and degrees of these needs! I have said that the baby cannot survive without having a nurturing mother, but this implies the obvious statement that the mother has a vested emotional interest in seeing her baby thriving, the proof positive of her nurturing abilities. As the baby grows from infant, to toddler, to an older and increasingly social being, this can present quite a challenge for some mothers. It is not so unusual for a mother to become broody as soon as her child joins nursery school. There may, of course, be many varied reasons for this, but one of them could be a sense of "losing" the child to teachers and peers.

An interesting response in the child may be brought out if the parents argue in front of him. Seeing his parents clashing with each other, the child will often "take sides", and usually he will turn to the parent he perceives to be in greater pain. No matter what each parent says or what any outsider might make of the situation, perhaps by natural instinct the child is driven to comfort the parent that he believes is hurt. But I suspect that this is one of those situations where it is impossible to decide what comes first—is it the child who turns to the hurt parent? Or is it the hurt parent who bids for the child's support?

The fact is that whenever we have a situation of dependence, *both* parties must have the ability and the wish to move away, to do without the other. In practice, this does not necessarily mean a physical parting but, rather, an emotional detachment. All parents will say that nothing gives them more pleasure and pride than seeing their offspring becoming independent. And yet it is not rare to find one of these parents feeling in some way "lost", disoriented, with no sense of purpose, virtually "abandoned" when the child goes to full-time school or, later, to university. In other words, I am trying to underline the fact that the child, like any other animal, is programmed to achieve an existence where he can be self-supporting, self-sufficient, independent of his parents. But it is also important to remember that this process requires each of the parents being able to let go of the child. Predictably, parents find this stage much easier to cope with when they can count on each other for the satisfaction of whatever "dependence" needs they have.

From an intellectual point of view, all these points seem clear and, hopefully, convincing. It is a shame that this clarity disappears when we are dealing with specific, real children and parents. Many of the assertions I have made can suddenly appear judgemental, virtually condemnatory, when addressed to, for example, the parents of a clinging child. Why should a toddler or an older child be afraid of going to school or to some other public, social place? Typically, we find that such a child has one parent who is forever criticizing him for his weakness, cowardice, or whatever, while the other parent is protective and comforting. When seen separately, as individuals, each of them may allow us to discover what the crisis means to him or her, and predictably the child's unconscious anxieties will rarely match the parents' perception of the situation. In my experience, virtually every phobic child turns out to be afraid not so much of *going somewhere* but, rather, of *moving away from home*. They may talk of home as the environment where they feel secure, but it takes little probing before it emerges that they have sensed that someone at home needs help. It is this finding that made clear to me the importance of the parents being able to let the child go, to move away from them.

However, we must keep in mind that we are not discussing mathematical equations. As a rule, that clinging, phobic child has siblings who present no such difficulties. It is therefore a question of discovering not simply *which child* is the parents' favourite, but what features in that particular child have led him to develop that specific problem.

Finally, I want to add a vital proviso: all the preceding discussion assumes that both child and parents are normally endowed to engage in a dependent relationship and, from there, to move on to independence—that is, being basically self-sufficient but still keeping feelings of togetherness and closeness. However, not everyone is born with this normal endowment. Whenever there is a physical or psychological disability, this inevitably has an effect on the nurturing, dependent mother–baby couple. When a child has a restricted capacity to become independent and self-sufficient, it is extremely difficult for the parents to gauge the ideal distance to keep between them and the child. Similarly, when there is an ill or incapacitated parent, the child too will find it very difficult to move away and build his own independent life.

When should a child start to be independent?

This question requires a qualification: "independent—according to whose judgement?" So often we can have a child or an adolescent claiming that he is independent—that is, able to look after himself—whereas parents or other outsiders may consider him as quite incapable of leading his life without some external source of support. Perhaps we should leave out the subjective, experiential factor and concentrate on the idea of the child's independence as seen from the parents' (or any observer's) perspective.

At birth, the human infant is in a situation of total dependence. He will only survive if properly looked after, a fact that was beautifully and poignantly defined by Donald Winnicott when he said that there's no such thing as a baby, only a baby and his mother. But as the infant grows, development is characterized by a multitude of minor and major steps that, fundamentally, signal his move towards independence from his caretakers. Being able to hold the bottle and later the spoon, acquiring language, tying up shoelaces—these are some of the markers of a growing capacity to engage in activities without assistance. When the toddler moves away from the parent and explores his environment, again we have signs of his increasing ability to extend his horizons away from his elemental source of security. This process carries on step by step, with some steps that are easily noticed and many others that tend to be missed or ignored.

A most important factor in this developmental process is the mother's reaction to the child's moves towards independence. I mentioned earlier (p. 10) the experiment with the baby crawling on a glass table top, where, most remarkably, if the mother displays a look of alarm, the baby freezes and stops or crawls back, but if she smiles warmly, the baby resumes his movements forwards, towards her. In another experiment with toddlers, precisely the same thing was found: when playing in a room, the child will move around freely but, every now and again, will look back to where his mother is. If she smiles encouragingly, he moves on—but if she has an expression of disapproval, the child stops and steps back towards her. What these experiments show is the extent to which a child's steps towards independence are intimately linked to the parent's ability to tolerate the child's moving away.

There is an element of art in parents' ability to enable their child to move towards independence. It is very easy to say: "Come on, you can do this by yourself now." But so much depends on the way these words are uttered and, even more subtly, on the whole gamut of attitudes that precede, accompany, and follow these words! The parents cannot predict how the child will react to their advice; they can only analyse their own position vis-à-vis that particular situation. Sometimes the parent will set out to be supportive and encouraging, only to find that the child reacts as if the parent had dealt him a painful, rejecting blow. It is important to be aware of our objectives, but we also have to assess the child's abilities and needs—continuously, repeatedly, since they can change without our having noticed this to be the case. I remember a mother spoon-feeding her baby; at one point he began to cry and turned his head away from the spoon. After trying twice to get her spoon accepted, the mother's intuition led her to change course: she put the spoon down and hugged the baby, murmuring loving words. The baby quietened down, sighed a few times, burying his head in his mother's breasts, and was soon ready and happy to resume eating his food.

A similar situation would take quite a different form with an older child: you want your child to make his way to school on his own (e.g., on foot or bicycle, by bus or train). But the child is reluctant: he cries, he clings to you, he speaks of dangers, he tells you of physical symptoms or asks you to postpone it for another day. How do you react? Clearly, there are two sides to this scenario: on the one hand your personal preference (convenience or necessity for yourself, now that your child is old enough to make the journey by himself), on the other the anxiety underlying the child's behaviour. The child may be afraid you want to get rid of him, or he may be dealing with the expectation that some danger might befall him on the way to school (perhaps something he saw on television or overheard in the playground). If you are not totally convinced of the need for the child to make the journey on his own and therefore either agree to let him stay at home or take him to school yourself, you may be giving him "evidence" that there are dangers from which he needs to be protected. If, on the other hand, you dig in your heels and demand that he goes off on his own, he may "decide" that, much as he feared, you want to get rid of him. If you now take into account that most of these fears are unconscious, you will recognize why I mentioned that helping the child to achieve self-sufficiency constitutes an art. The way of dealing with these situations is extraordinarily simple to spell out but enormously difficult to implement: you have to try to enable the child to recognize and reveal (articulate if possible) what upsets him. If, instead, you embark on a confrontation, I am afraid you will both have a lot of anguish and pain to contend with.

These examples may perhaps not be very convincing, but they are representative of the steps that lead a child from dependence on his parents to true independence. My definition of this is the child's self-sufficiency fully accompanied by the sense of a deep bond linking him to his parents. Independence does definitely not demand isolation; conversely, closeness need not mean intrusion, dependence, and humiliation.

Going back to that "when?" from a psychological point of view the child is ready to take steps towards independence, I would say that, taking into account his developmental capacities, the child should always be given the age-appropriate degree of independence. In real life, however, each family has its own concept of "independence". In some communities the child will be expected to have a job from quite early on, though that child's rights over his earnings will again vary from family to family. To take a more contentious example: at what age is a girl entitled to find herself a partner or a husband? If you then take into account the question of arranged marriages, what does this imply in terms of independence? And the role in which women are cast in some societies? Surely, the examples can be multiplied endlessly! Therefore, the conclusion is obvious: only each couple, each mother and father, can really decide when their child should be considered independent. Easy? Not entirely, as we can verify by checking what happens in families where children are going through adolescence. The teenager is given a room: wonderful! But who decides when the room should be cleaned? A daughter buys herself some clothes that father considers totally immoral—but mother thinks it is only fair she should experiment with her looks. How do parents respond when their son asks for money to buy a car? And what if parents decide that once they reach a certain age, their children should find independent accommodation? Or the other way around: parents who make the children live in the parental home until they get married!

I may well have created some confusion with my answers! But if, as a parent, you need any consolation, do try to remember that your child also has exactly the same difficulties in deciding the extent to which he wants to be independent: that is, the precise constraints of what is involved in his wanting to be treated as an independent person.

Will what I say or do help my child learn to become his own person? Or will he just see it as meddling?

From the child's point of view, it is always possible that any intervention by the parents will be taken as "meddling". We can never guess whether we will hear a "thank you" or exactly the opposite, so there is no point in trying. Having said this, it is quite likely that each one of us will have a clear expectation of how he is likely to react each time we address him. Children and parents create patterns and build assumptions about each other's styles, motives, and intentions, and this cannot but influence the way in which each of them addresses the other. It is part of living together that parents will never stop giving advice, requests, or commands, and, by definition, children have to react to these communications. Their reaction will be determined by how they feel about the parent's intervention (content, timing, tone of delivery, etc.), and this feeling depends on a great number of other factors.

To "become his own person" describes the process through which the child moves from being dependent on his parents to becoming an independent adult. As described earlier, the newborn infant is seen as totally dependent on his environment, and gradually he acquires the capacity to provide for himself, until the point is reached when he becomes self-sufficient and independent.

Considering another description of this process, we postulate that at birth the infant has no awareness of being an individual, a self-contained, complete, integral human being. Research has shown that already in his first days of life the infant uses his senses to react to environmental stimuli, but we still lack evidence of how he *experiences* these reactions. Theories have been formulated that describe evolving stages whereby the baby comes to recognize that he is separate from an *other* being outside his self. The very process of achieving awareness of what constitutes his *self* is considered one of enormous complexity. A small example: at which point will the infant distinguish between his thumb and his mother's nipple? Observing a baby, we can see that the first time his thumb finds its way into his mouth, he will stop crying and suck his thumb; after a while the crying is resumed until the breast (or bottle) appears on the scene. It is a matter of weeks before we observe the infant using his thumb as any other kind of dummy, while he will cry hard when it is food that he wants. Presumably, we can now speculate that the baby has learnt to distinguish between a nipple or teat that offers hunger-satiating stuff and something else that goes into his mouth and can soothe a different urge to suck. If the baby is also able to differentiate between the dummy and his thumb, then we would hypothesize that he has learnt that the thumb is something that he can control with particular movements of parts of his body. This apparently trivial difference between the dummy and the thumb is only an initial step in a major process of his discovering the parts of his body and the fact that they respond to his commands.

As the baby grows and his physiological capacities become richer and stronger, we will find endless examples of his learning new skills. Every single developmental step is considered to depend on a combination of innate factors and ones supplied by the environment. It is enormously important to keep track of the contribution of each of these factors, but in practice this only becomes an important issue when something is found to be deficient or faulty in the child's development.

Somehow, the child "becoming his own person" is an expression used only when the child disobeys the adults, but in fact this process has been going on from birth. The reason we do not see him as "his own person" is, of course, because he is learning the millions of things we teach him without putting up any particular objection. Most people who are familiar with small children growing up will know that each child has his own style of displaying what he has learnt from those around him. Children who tend to question what we teach them are described as stubborn, defiant, or querulous or as having strong personalities, depending on whom they interact with. Those who address or respond to us in the precise manner we expect of them are seen as sweet, quiet, easy, compliant, or having weak personalities, again depending on who is dealing with them. Logically, this is quite unrelated to the child's own experience of his relationship with the world, but it will have become clear from my answers to previous questions that I believe that, in practice, these epithets have an immense power to affect the child's self-image. This is because, at an unconscious level, the child comes to believe that *this* is how the parents expect him to behave. Somehow, a child seen as "sweet and compliant" can gradually turn into someone quite incapable of voicing any objection to the adults around him, much as another child praised for having "a strong personality" can gradually become a most objectionable, contentious troublemaker. It is children caught in extreme forms of this dynamic pattern that tend to pose formidable problems when one tries to assess how much in their personalities and attitudes is part of their innate endowment or, alternatively, a role they have learnt to play.

It is usually very difficult to establish with any precision the exact contribution of innate and environmental factors to the way in which the child faces the world. It is easy to say: "Well—with parents *like that*, what could you expect from the child?", but whenever it is necessary to ascertain the real potential of the child, this can be a dangerous oversimplification. In practice, what a parent must hold on to is the fact that when all is well and the child develops normally, nobody bothers to speculate about what comes from where . . .

I have not really answered the more difficult part of the question—that is, the parents' side of all these interactions. It is a fact that we will never find a parent who does not wish his child to grow and develop into a mature, independent human being. Some parents may joke about the "good old days" when the child obeyed them, much as other parents express sadness when their adolescent children speak about leaving home. But even these parents will firmly deny wanting to keep the children "tied to their apron strings". However, to quote a fairly common finding once again, there are mothers who become depressed when their children start school full-time and fathers who feel a great loss when their daughters announce that they have found a boy-friend. After all, each one of us will probably experience some degree of sadness at the same time as we celebrate our children's moves towards independence. Children have powerful antennae, and they desperately want to be loved and to gain their parents' approval of their moves out into the world; this means that they will always watch their parents' reactions to them very carefully. Here, then, is the challenge for the parents: to experience their reaction to the child's behaviour and yet be able to censor it, so that the child does not sense that elusive, subtle, but complex "disapproval" that they may be tempted to express.

A recent example comes to mind. An 18-month-old baby ate every meal while sitting on the lap of one of the parents or the nanny. One day, when visiting relations, a high-chair was offered to the family. When the child was put into the chair almost against the parents' wishes, he promptly picked up a spoon and fed himself quite energetically and incredibly dexterously. And at the following meal? A parent's lap again! It was very clear indeed that the parents found it very difficult to see their child demonstrating so vigorously its capacity for self-sufficiency.

Perhaps an amusing anecdote fits in here. A child never spoke, and the parents found themselves consulting no end of specialists—paediatricians, ear, nose, and throat specialists, neurologists, speech therapists: nothing worked. The child was now 8 years old, and one day he developed a very high temperature. The mother was very concerned and gave him the pre-scribed medication. When he was improving, one day she decided to give him some hot milk. As soon as she got near his bed and offered him the glass, the boy screamed: "Take that skin off! You know I hate milk skin!" The mother began to cry—she was *so* happy! "But, then, thank God, you *can* speak! How wonderful!" After a couple of minutes, she regained control of herself and asked the obvious question: "But if you can speak, why didn't you do so before?" "Because I never needed to. . . ."

I think this is a wonderful tale, but at the same time it makes the rather painful point that as long as a parent is prepared to do things that should, really, be undertaken by the child, this will delay the child's acquisition of that skill. Other parents operate at the opposite end of the scale, expecting their children to perform tasks for which they are not yet equipped. I suppose the simplest example is leaving their child alone while they go out, or putting him in charge of difficult chores or delicate or expensive things or his younger brothers and sisters and disregarding the possibility that he might feel anxious about this. Some children can cope, even if at the price of maturing prematurely, but others may develop symptoms as a protection. The irony here is that the moment the child is seen as phobic, anxious, or even just pathetic, the parents may accuse him of trying to blackmail them into not leaving him alone. To compound this unfortunate scenario, virtually every child like this blames himself for making his parents change their plans, and he feels guilty and ashamed for not being able to cope with the parents' original injunction. Over time the situation worsens, and when the parents finally decide to consult a specialist, it will have long ceased to be a question of demands that are beyond the child's abilities. Instead, he will be seen as a child who has learnt to use his neurosis to dominate and control his parents.

It is easy enough to advise parents to respect their child's autonomy and growing ability to deal with the world, but in practice it is very difficult to help them to gauge the precise balance of closeness and distance that would give the child optimum scope for development. Is any advice possible? The only advice I feel able to offer is that when the child says "I can't do it . . .", instead of excusing him or just saying "I *know* you can", perhaps it might pay to ask him: "Why not?" You may be lucky and remember some occasion when he did perform some similar task; in that case you can remind him of that situation. At the end of this dialogue, if he still claims "I can't!" you might try to turn it into a job for two people and suggest you do the task together. In fact, if you are absolutely certain the child can do it and you happen to feel in a very good mood, then it is well worth bursting out in a huge smile or laughter and say the classical, "Of course you can! I *know* you can!"

The real trouble with the child "becoming his own person" arises when he challenges principles, routines, and injunctions that are part of our notion of family life. The friendships he keeps, the food he eats (especially if contrary to a religious or other specific diet), style of dressing, manners at table, observance of religious stipulations—there is no end of examples here. Sooner of later, we have to face instances of self-expression as challenges and tests of our capacity to tolerate our child diverging from our own beliefs and behaviours. You will have found in your own circle of friends many examples of similar situations, and we all know how they can develop from trivial and commonplace arguments into huge dramas that bring pain to all involved.

The fact remains that if a child claims the right to self-expression and we are convinced that he is exposing himself to danger, we have to protest.

What happens next is, in truth, unpredictable. Our "rebellious" child can suddenly take our advice, much as the life-long "sweet" child can overnight become the irresponsible rebel. These are extremely difficult confrontations, and here I have a very firm piece of advice: *never*, just never, give up the fight. In my experience, adolescents will always protest, swear, fight against "dominating" parents, but I have found more casualties among those whose parents gave up on them. It seems that as long as we fight and persist in trying to make our principles clear, adolescents experience at an unconscious level that we value them sufficiently to carry on battling with them. Perhaps paradoxically, this seems to be seen as a statement of trust and a vote for their ability to cope with difficult situations. In contrast to this, when the parents withdraw, the adolescent seems to experience this not as a sign of respect, but as a vote of no confidence, a withdrawal of bonds, which leaves them totally alone, cut off from their base. Not that any adolescent would admit to this interpretation, but it is what my experience has taught me. Independence is always desirable, but when experienced as isolation and a position of having no place and no one to fall back on, in case of need, then this spells disaster.

When is a child "too good"?

A child is not usually seen as "too good" by his own parents: this is an assessment that tends to be made by outsiders. If we believe that a child is definitely "too good", then there is a chance that his parents see him as wonderfully co-operative, well-mannered, consistently positive and responsive, and so forth. His teachers may complain that he will never stand up for himself or that he allows others to bully him, forever turning the other cheek to be bullied again, and so on. Sometimes other teachers will describe the same child as well-behaved, co-operative, a delight to have as a pupil. When a child gives rise to these comments, there is a possibility that he may be "too good". This would describe a child who is able to sense what is expected of him and proceeds to embody, to fulfil, those expectations. This is an unconscious process, and most children with this psychological configuration would deny that they were being "too good": such an admission would be experienced as indicating a lack of sincerity, of genuineness, as if they were hypocritically feigning obedience, loyalty, or devotion.

I remember a friend of mine once telling his youngest son that he would be relieved and pleased the day the boy told him to get off his back. He felt that the son was just too concerned not to cause problems for his parents. He was aware of how much any disagreements between himself and his wife affected their son, and he thought this was interfering with the son's developing sense of independence, making him too self-conscious and compliant. Apparently, there were no immediate effects from these words aimed at "liberating" the son, but in later years that youngster built a life and career that involved living at a considerable geographic distance from his parents. This probably showed that he found a way of dealing with his unconscious compulsion to act as a peacemaker between the parents.

For a child to become "too good", there must be a definitely significant environmental factor, but this alone will never shape that child's character. The child must also possess some individual ingredient that matches that parental input. This can be seen in a family with several children. There is always a "Daddy's favourite" and a "Mummy's darling", but being a favourite child is still not the same as becoming "too good". Sometimes these "favourite children" are precisely the ones who create the most trouble! The "too-good" child may happen to be one of the favourites, but this is not necessarily the case. The "too-good child" is the one who will keep company with the parent running a temperature, the one who will not mind calling off meeting up with his friends when a parent needs help with some chore, the one who will ask only once for that biscuit or other morsel, never making trouble by insisting that he wants "only one more", the child who will stop anything he is doing when reminded that homework needs finishing and who will not linger when it comes to bedtime . What factors bring such behaviour into being? There must be a parental contribution, but there must also be a special constitutional endowment for the child to develop this role.

If this child goes into psychotherapy, there is a good chance that he may come to understand the unconscious motivation for his attitude to his parents and the world, and he may be able to change. But it is very important to work with the parents of this child alongside his therapy, to ensure that they can live with a child who treats them in a less "good" way. The parents have to discover the ways in which they contributed to the continuation of that "too-good" pattern. They must be told that this is not a question of blaming them for the child's way of being, but of helping them to contribute to the process of change in the child. If the parents cannot accept this, then it may be quite difficult for the child to improve. In practice, if parents cannot accept that a child should change through therapy, this enterprise is quickly brought to a halt.

It is important at this point to mention another concept that Donald Winnicott put on the map: the "false self". He described children who lived with parents who did not allow them to build on their "natural" potentials. These children adapted to the situation by unconsciously developing attitudes and behaviours that the parents could approve of. Note the word *unconsciously*! Winnicott is not referring to a clever stratagem, to a deliberate deception where a façade is created. He found patients who presented with a personality structure that subsequently proved to be a cover for sentiments, thoughts, and attributes that had become hidden and unavailable to that person. These "true" attributes of that patient's self seemed to have been repressed, relegated into the unconscious, in an attempt to live in the environment experienced by the patient while growing up. Though it is quite possible that some of the "false-self" patients might have been "too-good" children, I suspect that Winnicott's concept was meant to describe a wider range of characters. My reading of his work suggests that a "false self" might also, for example, signify a façade of disturbed behaviour where the "real self" was, in fact, better balanced and stable. This is the reason why my description of the "too-good" child was not restricted to quoting Winnicott's work.

When is a child "too naughty"?

You know your child really is "too naughty" when, contrary to your good, parental judgement, you wish you could strangle him! To *you*, it is indisputable that the child's behaviour is intolerable. When a teacher keeps punishing a child or complains about him, this means that *he* believes that the child is "too naughty". Why, though, are you in this case most likely to suspect that there is something wrong *with* the teacher or *between* him and your child?

Naughtiness is a personal judgement: it cannot possibly be measured. This is why to an outsider a complaint of "excessive naughtiness" is very often taken as a reflection on the complainant rather than on the child. As we well know, quite often when a parent complains that his child is incredibly insubordinate, there is someone who will say, in the sweetest possible tone of voice, "But with me, he is such a lovely child!"

We live in times when "too naughty" children are often referred for an assessment to check whether they have Attention Deficit Hyperactivity Disorder (ADHD). Many professionals, however, dispute the validity of this diagnosis: some argue that this is another instance of our present trend to "medicalize" daily life; others are suspicious of all diagnoses made on the basis of checklists; and others still will point out that ADHD is only a descriptive diagnosis, not a disease. On the other hand, some parents cannot tolerate uncertainties and may welcome a clear diagnosis that an authority claims to be an explanation for the behaviour that worries them. There is no doubt whatever that some children with this diagnosis *do* improve with appropriate medication, but not all do so. This suggests that ADHD is something of an umbrella diagnosis, encompassing many different pathological entities, but then also providing a convenient way of attributing a medical origin to the worrying behaviour of children who may well prove to be quite normal. We will need many more years before we can sharpen our diagnoses of this group of children.

ADHD amalgamates what were originally two different clinical pictures; over time, the two diagnoses have merged, since so many children present difficulties that cover both fields. Attention Deficit Disorder (ADD) described children who cannot concentrate for any length of time and have considerable learning difficulties of various kinds. They often seem to switch off and "live in a world of their own", and this can happen whether they are on their own or working or playing with an adult. The "H" stands for hyperactivity, referring to children who are restless, have sleeping difficulties, and behave in a manner that baffles most people around them, since their continual movements often appear random and unfocused. There are, of course, ordinary children who appear to have inexhaustible resources of energy and are described as energetic, vigorous, determined, and the like. By contrast, hyperactive children become the object of attention because they have an apparent underlying level of anxiety and their movements seem to follow a logic that escapes those around them. In fact, very often, when asked to explain what they are doing or why they do it, these children may come up with a "don't know", charged with varying degrees of puzzlement.

But coming back to the question under consideration, most of these children will qualify for the "too-naughty" label. However cynical or regrettable it might seem, two children with precisely the same symptomatology will receive whichever label—"ADHD" or just "lively"—predominates in the area where they live; in some other cultures that same child might even qualify for the label of "possessed". The point I am trying to make is that at the end of the day, as far as your child is concerned, it is your view that counts. It can happen that in your household everybody and everything operates at high speed, and/or members of the family are supposed to have clear, personal opinions; in other words, taking things easy is seen as laziness, and conformity or submission are seen as a sign of weakness, so having views and being able to voice them—preferably in forceful, loud terms—is seen as a virtue to be encouraged. The next-door neighbours may value a quiet atmosphere within the household, where words are whispered and opinions are to be expressed only when requested. It is obvious that these two families will define "naughtiness" in two totally different ways. In practice, it is usually the parents who decide that professional assistance is to be sought. What follows is that, for better or for worse, it is the combined view of parents and professionals that will dictate what happens to the child. Only time can tell whether the child was "rescued" and given treatment that ensures the full realization of his potentials, or was, instead, subjected unnecessarily to investigations resulting from the anxieties of the adults in his world.

How can I tell what is bothering my child? Could it be depression?

For the sake of your peace of mind, I would suggest you forget the word "depression". Over the last two or three decades the psychiatric and paediatric worlds have adopted this diagnosis with a fierce passion. Papers and books have been written, and children are put through sophisticated diagnostic assessments and sometimes even put under medication. Much as with ADHD and a wide range of behavioural and educational difficulties, a great deal of attention is being given to children in trouble. This is not the place to discuss what many people see as the "medicalization" of common human problems, nor do I want to debate to what extent we are justified in diagnosing a depressive illness in childhood. It is important that doctors should discuss among themselves the differences between an illness called "depression" and those mood and temperament variations that include depressed feelings, but parents are looking for trouble if they get involved in these issues. I would remind you of the obvious fact that doctors see only those children who are brought to them. This fact is used frequently these days to emphasize that children who need and could benefit from help are being deprived of medical attention. But the other side of this same coin is that many "depressed" children are brought to see a doctor by parents who might be able to help their children were they given appropriate help for themselves. So instead of arguing over these fascinating issues, I would propose a different approach.

Rather than wondering whether your child is depressed, I suggest instead that you wonder whether he is unhappy. I have no doubt whatsoever that you need no help to recognize unhappiness in another human being, let alone in your own child. This approach might allow you to implement a helping programme rather than worrying whether you should consult your doctor. *First rule of thumb*: rather than waiting for your child to tell you that he feels unhappy, you should feel totally free to ask him something like, "You don't look your usual self—is anything wrong?" Depending on the child's age, it is quite likely that the only reaction you will get is a shrug of the shoulders or some puzzling grimace. *Second rule of thumb*: until you have proof to the contrary, assume that this reaction is an unconscious way of testing the degree of interest you have in discovering how he is feeling. If all you then do is grunt and move away, then that is the end of that round. Ideally, you should instead voice a further sympathetic phrase—something like "I wish I could understand what your shoulders are saying" or "I guess you don't know what to say . . . but I really think you don't seem so happy today" (always "you *don't know*", and not "you *don't want*"). Some children may say something meaningful now—others are more resistant. If there is still no answer forthcoming, perhaps you can round off your attempt by saying that you hope you've got the wrong impression—but, "If I'm right and there really is something bothering you, please do tell me whenever you feel it is the right time." *Third*—and most important—*rule of thumb*: if and when your child comes to tell you what is bothering him, you simply *must* be careful not to explain it away. However silly, childish, illogical, obvious, or plainly stupid it might be, don't give a suggestion, supply an answer, offer a different or better way of "looking at it", try to correct some "wrong interpretation", or make any other similar input. Each of these is bound to be felt by the child as your way of shutting him up, not taking him seriously, not really wanting to know what is bothering him. My Rule 3 recommends that you should try to find a way of putting a question back to the child: "What makes you say that?" "Who told you so?" "Are you really sure?" "Can you explain this to me?" "I understand what you said, but there is that bit [quote it!] that escapes me: what do you mean?" With luck, the child may venture further information.

My approach is based on a fundamental belief that you might not actually agree with: the vast majority of unhappy children are not really clear about the precise nature of what makes them so unhappy. They grab hold and tell you of events or interactions that they believe might be relevant, but even then they may not be able to articulate the reason why this is upsetting them. In view of my theory, I am suggesting that rather than reassuring the child, you try to help him to figure out gradually, by himself, what might be making him unhappy. I do very strongly believe that your demonstration of interest is the best reassurance you might ever give your child.

Back to your question: do you really need me to explain how you can recognize that your child is "depressed"? I doubt it. I certainly think that it is an exception for a child to get to the point of requiring a psychiatric interview to elucidate whether he is depressed. Another word about this: if your attempts to "break through" do not succeed, do consider the possibility of getting your spouse or one of the grandparents or another relative you trust to try to get the child to open up to them. This may work, particularly if, unknown to you, your child believes that you are yourself going through some bad patch: no child will ever confide problems to a parent if he believes that he is going to make the parent's situation worse.

If you discover that your child is unhappy because he is worried about you, then this raises a very difficult problem: how much should you tell him about what is, in fact, making *you* unhappy? After all, parents also have problems of their own, and, worse still, they can experience periods of depression. I fear there is no general principle to cover these possibilities. You might be upset because of your spouse's behaviour (in which case the child may well have some idea that this is the reason for your mental state), you may be struggling with the diagnosis of some medical condition, or some loved relation may be fatally ill—the possibilities are endless. But above all, your reaction to being confronted by your child's spotting your unhappiness will depend on your personality. Some people do not mind sharing their worries or might even like to do so, others will not do it whatever the pressures they are subjected to. If you are aware of being upset, worried, or depressed, the most important thing is to respect your own limits: do not go against these "for the sake of your child", because there is a good chance that you will end up resenting him for making you break your principles. The best way out is to consider the child's age and find out very carefully how much he really wants to, and can, take in: sometimes stating that you are not well but that things are being sorted out is enough to reassure a younger child. The older child will have learnt that certain subjects are not to be raised in the family: these will vary from one family to another, but all of us have a range of topics that we consider totally private and simply never to be considered as subjects for general discussion.

If you happen to be struggling with issues related to these subjects, it is even more important not to let the child know of these thoughts. By the time children reach the age of 4 or 5 years, they will take it for granted that there are subjects that are not spoken about in the family, even if they can be seen or heard at school, in the neighbourhood, or on television.

But I must repeat: put yourself first. If you are going through a bad patch, however much you want to help your child with his unhappiness, try to enlist someone else's help. As long as this person is someone you trust, there is a much better chance that both you and your child will obtain the help you both need.

My daughter keeps biting her nails and hair: how can we get her to stop doing this?

Nail-biting and hair-biting or hair-pulling are well-recognized "nervous habits", and most parents try to break their child of such habits (although, perhaps understandably, parents who themselves bite their nails, say, are rather more tolerant of their children doing this). On the other hand, there are thousands of things that a child has to learn and that become natural, second nature, but we simply do not call them "habits": getting dressed, tying shoelaces, combing the hair, using a knife and fork, and so on—the list is very long! But if most parents now accept children holding on to favourite toys or dolls or blankets at bedtime, we still get concerned over other bedtime rituals. When is a "habit" a sign of anxiety, and when is it simply part of developing a personal style of living? Where should one draw a line?

The simplest answer is that parents will draw the line between acceptable and objectionable behaviour on the basis of their beliefs, whether these are well founded or the result of personal prejudices. There are people who are quite incapable of submitting their beliefs to scrutiny. We can call them impulsive, opinionated, big-headed, omnipotent, deluded, or any other adjective, but for better or for worse, they cannot help being how they are. People like this do not speak of hunches, intuition, beliefs; they claim certainties and convictions, and they proceed accordingly. When they become parents, their children will gradually adapt to a system of expectations that leaves little room for divergence or compromise. If both parents share these convictions, then it can become easier for the child to learn what will then be called "the family's way of life". This applies to cleanliness, table manners, dietary habits, religious rituals, and innumerable other aspects of daily living. If, instead, one of the parents has different views, then the child has a formidable challenge. Learning a particular way of tackling a task becomes a credit to one parent but may be taken as an act of defiance by the other. What the parents see as the child obeying or defying their injunctions signifies for the child a continuous state of uncertainty, if not insecurity. A rather common example is the child who wets himself instead of going to the toilet. One parent will feel angry and frustrated and demand a change in this behaviour, while the other will put forward mitigating circumstances. To put it at its simplest: going to the toilet when wanting to pass water ceases to be the "natural" way of emptying the bladder and becomes an instance of showing obedience or defiance to the parents. The word "natural" is important, as this emphasizes another instance of a piece of behaviour that is usually a totally automatic part of daily life being turned into a highly charged emotional situation.

All children will at some point develop their own individual way of dealing with anxiety, fear, or insecurity. Some children burst out crying, some faint, some begin to stammer, others hit out and hurt others or themselves. There is no point at all in trying to consider better or worse ways of dealing with this type of emotional breakdown, since most of us cannot but stick with what we have developed as our typical style of releasing, giving expression to, powerful feelings that overcome our capacity to think rationally. This does not happen out of a considered review of such episodes, but simply because we cannot help it. On the whole, it is the individual—adult as well as child!—who most wishes he were able to overcome these "nervous habits". However, only rarely will you find an individual prepared to admit this.

In practice, when faced with the problem of a child's nervous habit, we can only take our own responses into account—not necessarily immediately translating these into action but, rather, examining carefully what prompted that intuitive reaction. You tell me that your child is biting her nails and her hair, and you believe that she is obviously anxious about something. What leads you to believe this to be the case? As you know, other people (perhaps even your partner!) may say that this biting is a way of winding you up, much as another family will declare it a disgusting habit, carrying the danger of all kinds of contamination from the dirt. Therefore, it is important to recognize whether you interpret the habit as indicating anxiety because you can pick up other signs of anxiety in the child, or whether you are simply following another person's interpretation that you have heard or read. There is no point in telling the child that she is anxious just because someone else thought this was the case. On the other hand, if you spot that the hair- or nail-biting occurs immediately after some event that you know, from previous experience, tends to upset your child, you can refer to this rather than simply throwing at the child a question about what is "truly" upsetting her.

Children, exactly like adults, are not happy to admit to a sense of impotence. We all resort to face-saving behaviours in the hope that this will give us time to overcome the original sense of being thrown off balance. In the vast majority of cases there is quite a possibility that we won't even become conscious of what precisely unbalanced us! Being asked about it can only lead to a "don't know!" Can you imagine your friend's reaction if, on his lighting a cigarette, you ask him what has so upset him that he has resorted to a therapeutic fag? If, however, you noticed a hostile remark that somebody else in the group made about your friend, you can wink or nudge or even put into words your impression that this has got under your friend's skin. Perhaps he will still smoke his cigarette, but you might have opened the door to his actually putting into words what was upsetting him. In the case of your daughter, strategically, it is best to not make any direct reference to the biting but, instead, attempt to find a circuitous route to teach her that this habit may be a response to stimuli that hurt or upset her. I happen to believe that the vast majority of habits come to lose the specific meaning they may have possessed when they first started. Furthermore, as I wrote above, many of these habits become a highly personal form of self-comfort and reassurance. If I am correct, you will not manage to make your daughter stop her biting by addressing it "head-on". But if your intuition tells you that this habit has been triggered off by some anxiety and your sixth sense is correct, then your attempting to help your daughter to recognize her feelings will very probably make her feel comforted. A common example is that of the young child who reacts to the birth of a younger sibling as if this signified the loss of her loving mother: regressing to daytime or bedtime wetting, biting nails, sucking fingers can all become an unconscious testing-out of whether the mother is still prepared to comfort and nurture her in her needs. In such a case, your gentle inquiries are likely to be experienced as proof that your love is still the same. She may come to feel reassured enough to share with you what is frightening or worrying her. And if she does overcome her sense of insecurity, she may well give up the biting, discovering instead the alternative route of putting anxious feelings into words to someone who is loved and trusted.

My son fiddles with his genitals; I don't mind this at home, but it's embarrassing in public: what shall I do?

Your son fiddling with his genitals is a problem, but your second sentence represents a far greater and more complex problem. The clash between what is acceptable at home but is not to be displayed outside can come up in so many different formulations. Take immigrant families who speak one language at home, while adopting the local language when in outside society. Or the Jews at the time of the Inquisition in Spain, who kept an outward appearance of having abandoned their Jewishness while adhering to their practices within the domestic setting. Or the parent who swears relentlessly at any provocation but demands that his children should not repeat those words at school. The point of mentioning these various situations is to call your attention to the enormously challenging task of teaching your child the rationale behind such behaviours.

You can try to tell your child that "this" (whatever the problem) is what you demand he should comply with. Depending on his age and his personality, your child may ask you "why?" If you are the kind of parent who simply snaps back "because that is what I want!" you are safe and clear, though the chances are that your child will not ask you "why?" many times again, and it is by no means clear that he will obey you. But if you are, instead, the type of parent who enjoys a challenge and wants to foster your child's understanding of the world in which he lives, it is still not easy to convince a child of the importance of accepting your request. However, it is likely to be a rewarding effort.

As for fiddling with the genitals, I remember how my father dealt with my brother's doing this: "Are you afraid it will fall off?" he would ask. He didn't know about psychoanalytic theories, but his intuition and sense of humour were probably taking him in the right direction. Many boys do hold their penis or even masturbate as a means of disproving the unconscious anxiety that their penis might disappear. But in most cases where boys, or girls, are playing with their genitals, there is also an element of excitement and pleasure in the activity. I happen to believe that the way we (all of us!) are wired, it is very easy for a piece of behaviour to become a habit. This is significant only to the extent that, once a habit is formed, it becomes virtually devoid of meaning. If "fiddling with the genitals" starts as a response to a specific anxiety or represents an attempt to gain excitement that overshadows the anxiety, these particular meanings can get lost under the cover of a habit. Once this compulsive action sets roots, it does not seem to matter whether or not it is pleasurable, since the particular behaviour can occur the moment the child's anxiety threshold is crossed. This theory is illustrated by the joke of the man sitting at the bar, with a Scotch in front of him. "Why do you drink so much?" asks his friend. "Oh . . . to forget . . ." answers our man. "To forget what?" ". . . I've forgotten, actually" he answers, taking another gulp of Scotch.

The most common advice given in these situations is to say that you must not make "too much" of it, since it will only make your son move on to do it when not in your presence. But it is impossible for you to ignore it, since your child may, in fact, be (at least unconsciously) trying to find out how you respond to his behaviour. I would say that if your child is over 3 to 4 years old, then it is perfectly in order for you to explain to him that fiddling with his genitals is one of those things that are not supposed to be done in public. You might explain that people in different climates and circum- stances dress differently, because our body is sensitive to temperatures, and this leads to different degrees of covering one's body. But dressing aside, the body is there to be seen as a part of your person, and people do not expect to see you touching any part of it. In our society, if you stick your finger into your nose or if you decide to scratch your behind, people see this as disgusting or a sign of disrespect. In view of what children see on television, your boy may well remind you of images of women voluptuously moving their hands and arms over their head, chest, and groin. This is a difficult challenge, but you can only try to emphasize the difference be- tween those ballet-like movements and the actual handling of body parts. The nose, the behind, the penis are parts of the body that deal with things going in and out of the body, and this is seen by everyone as involving very private activities, not to be displayed in public.

If your child is under 3 years old, then you might choose to assume that fiddling with his genitals is an action aiming not at sexual gratification, but at avoiding some other thought or feeling. This idea would lead you to try to divert his attention with some toy or game or other activity. Such strategy would follow the recommendation of "not making much of it", while implic- itly hoping to get the message across to the child that you want him to stop playing with his genitals. If, however, you enjoy a good challenge, then I suggest you try to find that ideal moment when you and your child are alone, playing peacefully together, and then use various phrasings that might convey to the child that you believe there is something bothering him. No direct reference to the touching the genitals, picking the nose, or whatever habit the child is practising—the rationale here is to discover which words will enable the child to recognize that he may be harbouring *affects, anxieties,* that you are prepared to help with. With luck, the child may find ways of showing you, in words or through his games, what is making him feel anxious. The assumption is that the "habit" is a communication, one way of conveying to you that the child is struggling with feelings he cannot render in words.

* * *

Having discussed in these last two questions the problems of children touching parts of their bodies, it is important to mention that inappropriate touching can also occur when the child has an underlying medical problem, such as a bacterial, fungal, or parasitical infection, which may be producing intense discomfort. Particularly persistent touching may indicate an infection, and medical advice should then be sought.

3

Siblings and peers

Is rivalry between siblings normal?
What if it becomes inappropriate or excessive?
How can one be fair to both children?

To some extent, with sibling rivalry much depends on how old the children are. Take the toddler who bites or hits his new-born baby brother, and compare that with the story of the 8-year-old who dropped a heavy cast-iron pan onto the head of his baby brother asleep in the cot. I once heard of a 6-year-old girl who was found pulling the penis of her 18-month-old baby brother; she justified this by saying that she wanted to have it for herself. The first problem is whether you (and anyone else) would really agree that these are all instances of "sibling rivalry". If you do, it is still quite obvious that each of these examples calls for a totally different approach.

I want to make a gross generalization, but I really do believe it is valid to say that when "sibling rivalry" is displayed by a young child, this indicates that the "offender" is fighting to regain his place in the parents' hearts. We might go into a discussion on the precise difference between jealousy and envy, but perhaps we can agree that the toddler in my example is jealous of the baby for displacing him as the best-loved child and that the little girl is envious of her brother's penis. But the behaviour of the 8-year-old would demand a much closer analysis to elicit the causes for his attack on the baby.

Considering only my examples, it is easy enough to devise means of dealing with them. The parents of the toddler will need to find ways of reassuring him that their love is not diminished by the arrival of the baby. We might wish that this work had started long before the toddler felt threatened, but it does not follow that any parent can completely prevent such reactions in a young child. Hearing stories of toddlers who attack their

61

younger siblings, it is very easy to blame the parents, but we must always make allowances for individual factors that operate in each child. Indeed, these factors are affected by the way in which the parents teach and treat the child, but these individual elements still make a major contribution to each situation, even if they are far more difficult to identify.

Our little girl will require very clear explanations about gender differences. Again, you might say that these should have taken place years earlier—I would agree, but I would still repeat my argument that such incidents are not totally "the parents' fault". Many girls who have had endless lessons on anatomy and physiology may still find themselves harbouring the textbook "penis envy". This proves the point that teaching something is never, in itself, a guarantee that the pupil has the ability to absorb the data in exactly the manner intended by the teacher. As a psychoanalyst, I would be interested not only in the conscious "I want to have his penis", but in other ideas—conscious and unconscious—that led to that episode on that specific occasion. But such explorations are not to be undertaken by parents. It is best for the parents to explain what is involved and underline the pointlessness and inappropriateness of the particular behaviour. If the girl raises other reasons, these should be given proper attention, since they may well be very illuminating. A rule of thumb: ideally, the child should be asked questions, to have the chance to explain herself, make comments, and raise questions of her own. Explanations are necessary, but only after we have established what precisely is the child's quandary.

The attack by the 8-year-old is far more alarming. What made this episode particularly strange was to hear that the parents dealt with it by putting the baby somewhere else and replacing it in the cot by a big doll. How this would help the child, I fail to understand. The most difficult element in such a situation is to establish whether this is a one-off episode or whether it is a warning sign of more serious disturbance in the child. Certainly, whatever the parents' ingenuity may devise by way of remedying the problem, considering the age of the boy concerned I would certainly have urged them to get the child seen by a child specialist.

So much for examples. I could give more instances of sibling rivalry, but fundamentally we have to accept that human nature cannot be changed—and rivalry is an integral constituent of our make-up. I have yet to meet someone who never makes comparisons between himself and others around him. The difference is only that some will allow such comparisons to be known, while others keep them secret. We all crave recognition (love, really), but only some of us will allow this to become manifest. Self-esteem is part of our being, and we all gauge it, not only in self-centred terms, but through observations—overtly or covertly—of the others in the world around us. In a sense, we might say that whether it is rational or irrational, sibling rivalry is always part of normal life. When, however, a child makes us aware of his experiencing such feelings, it is important to offer him the help being requested. Obviously, our response depends on the manner in which these feelings are expressed, but though we have to impose limits on how the child behaves, we must not ignore the fact that such expressions of jealousy constitute a statement of feeling inferior, short-changed, or deprived. We must always protect the victim of any jealous attack from a sibling, but the perpetrator needs more than simply punishment or correction.

I forgot the word "inappropriate". Only rarely will a toddler express jealousy by telling one of his parents that they are giving the baby all the love that used to be given to him. . . . Every family with two or more children has seen a toddler asking for some of the baby's bottle or dummy or whatever. Every single toddler will wriggle his way onto mother's lap when she is holding the baby. The examples are endless! But I imagine the word "inappropriate" only comes on the scene when someone is hurt or runs the risk of being hurt. Perhaps it is difficult to know the extent to which the aggressor can obey our injunctions, but it is terribly important to show him what is acceptable behaviour and what is not. To state the obvious, this "setting the boundaries", as it is called nowadays, will vary in form and style from one family to the next, but it is a vital ingredient in teaching the child how his family lives.

Why does my son bite his big sister, though usually they play happily together? How can I put a stop to it?

As you will have gathered, I take a very simplistic view of problems like this. Many of my psychoanalytic colleagues would emphasize your son's use of his mouth and speak of "hostile oral impulses". In Freud's theory of emotional development, the mouth is seen as the earliest point of contact between infant and mother, and therefore the external world, the others. Freud put forward a theory where "instincts" were a fundamental force that moved the individual in his struggle for survival. It made sense, therefore, to look at development in terms of the various stages where different parts of the body appeared to be the main point of contact—input and output—with the child's environment. Freud postulated that the oral phase covered the child's first year of life. During the second year, the "anal phase" became the more important one, in view of the toilet-training process: the child's body has matured to achieve muscular control, and the environment expects the child to be clean. This is followed by the phallic phase, in which the child becomes aware of his genitals and their functions, the time when gender identity tends to take shape. As you can see, this is an attempt to bring the biological framework of concepts into the otherwise psychological concepts that characterize the psychoanalytic body of theories. An important element of the theory is that these instincts are supposed to be invested with an emotional charge, which allows us to differentiate between constructive and destructive uses of the instincts. Focusing, then, on your child's biting, this might be seen as a hostile use of the physiological action of biting, which, when used for eating, would signify a constructive application of the instinct.

I prefer to look at the "biting the sister" from quite a different perspective. I draw a sharp distinction between the first time when biting occurs and the subsequent ones. Conceivably, something happened between your children that led the boy to feel a wish to hurt his sister (I cannot imagine any other emotional content for the physical movements involved in biting another person!). Why he bit her, rather than using his fists or feet, I cannot explain. But I would assume that his sister's reaction made him realize that his objective had been attained and, what is more important, that behaviour of that kind did not lead to any intolerable and undesirable consequences. Using different words, I cannot explain how it came to happen for the first time, but seeing that the biting was repeated, then I take it that your son did not register any sense that this biting was unacceptable and never to be done again.

I see your son's biting as an expression of a particular set of emotions that in another child might have been expressed in endless other ways. Your daughter's reaction would have been experienced as an implicit agreement that that particular mode of expression of her brother's feelings could be used again. If you ask how you can stop it, I think it is important to speak to your daughter and try to understand why she has not reacted in an effective self-protective way. Actually, I see this as much more important than your son's biting! Your daughter has to be helped to defend herself not just from her younger brother (who, you say, loves and plays with her), but from all other children whom she will meet at school and elsewhere.

I think all that your son needs is a good reprimand, a clear message that this biting is not acceptable—particularly not in your family. I mean you must say "*Stop!*" and definitely not "Stop, *please!*" I don't believe in "biting back" or other similar techniques. If your son does not respond to the firm admonishment I suggested, then there may be more complex issues involved. It may be difficult for you as a parent to probe, to find the right questions that will enable him to give you more clues to work out what ideas and impulses lead him to hurt his sister. However futile it seems, it is still worth telling him that in your family people *voice* their feelings. Whatever else, you must teach him that biting is not allowed. Ideally, he should be helped to find his own way to recognize how the wish to hurt comes to overpower him and leads him to bite someone he is so close to. If you find that your boy stops biting but becomes silent or withdrawn or sad, this would suggest that he is able to obey you, but that he is still struggling with feelings that require attention. In this case, it might be useful to consult a professional in your local child guidance clinic.

One child has special needs, the other is "normal" : how can parents manage?

What a nightmare! Parents have always liked to boast that "all my children are equal in my eyes! I love each of them just as much as I love the others!" Even if we were to assume that this could ever be true, we still have to take it for granted that every single child has a very clear conviction of which sibling is "Daddy's favourite" or "Mummy's little jewel". I suspect every child will weave some kind of explanation to justify his not being the favourite or, to put it more accurately, why the one he considers to be the favourite has come to occupy that position.

It is a bit of a mystery to me to define the point at which children begin to make comparisons with siblings. Following closely the events when a new baby arrives home, there is no doubt that any older children observe the baby's day-to-day life. My impression, however, is that the new arrival is much more "disturbing" to a toddler than to a school-age child. An older child, particularly girls, will tend to "offer their services" to the mother, and in many families this older daughter may even assume the position of a second mother; boys, on the whole, tend to get out of the way as much as possible . . . But the situation is very different when the older child is a toddler: here, there is a clear atmosphere of insecurity. Obviously, we have to make allowances for the older child's age, but initially, most toddlers seem to relate not to the baby himself, but to "Mummy's new baby": in other words, even when touching or trying to play with the new arrival, it is the mother's reaction that the toddler appears to be scrutinizing. We can only assume that the toddler is trying to ascertain whether the new baby has taken his mother away from him. At this point, there is no question of the baby's characteristics being at all important, and it is the mother's handling of the toddler's exploratory approaches that seem to make a lot of difference in shaping the toddler's attitude to the new baby.

I would be hard put to guess at which point these comparisons that we subsume under the label "sibling rivalry" take into account one child's "giftedness" or, conversely, disability. It is easy enough to assume that the child has to have reached a level of awareness of another child's (higher or lower) competence before we can consider this a relevant factor in the relationship between the siblings. Even then, I believe it would be quite difficult to establish whether the rivalry was directed at the other sibling or, again, against the parents who seem to give the child that extra bit of care and attention.

But your question refers to the way in which the parents should handle these situations. I can only repeat: this is a nightmarish issue. I am sure that all parents want to care for their children in such a manner that none of them feels short-changed in any way and, at the same time, that ensures that the children will treat each other as equals, irrespective of each child's needs and abilities. But the point will always be reached when a child's individual capacities will demand appropriate, special care. A deaf child will probably require a special school, much as a gifted musician may deserve placement at a distant music school.

Thinking of families that I have observed, two of them might be mentioned. In one, the older, very bright girl mercilessly tormented the younger girl, who was of low-average intelligence. The parents alternately punished her and coaxed and encouraged her to treat her sister less contemptuously, but to no avail. In another family, both an older and a younger sibling treated a middle child, who had a severe intellectual disability, with extreme love and care. I tend to think that the parents' attitude to each child is very important—above all at very early stages, right when any disability or special gift first becomes apparent. By the time such families see a professional, it is usually impossible to ascertain whether the relationship between siblings is linked to parental influences or whether they result from each child's feelings about the sibling.

In practice, whether the "special" child is older or younger than his siblings, the only thing the parents can do is to reassure each child that their (parental) love is not contingent on their abilities, but that each child has a guaranteed place in both parents' hearts. Easier said than done, since the result of the parents' efforts depends so much on each child's psychological make-up. Sooner or later, disability or giftedness will require appropriate handling, but I still believe that most children can tolerate a sibling's special needs if they can feel secure in their position within the family. However, over and above the parents' ministrations, each child has his own perception of his abilities and those of the special sibling—and this leads to a much more complex picture.

The issues here refer to each child's self-image and self-esteem. However important the parents' role, in the context of giftedness and special needs there is a limit to how much parents can affect each child's perception of himself and of his siblings. As the years go by, so many other factors come to influence their lives that it can be difficult to establish the precise relevance of the earliest parental input.

I have been discussing this issue as it affects children growing up, but perhaps I should mention something of what I have found when meeting some of these children in adult life. Early on, as the giftedness is discovered, it is a fact that it demands adaptation from each member of the family—and there is no doubt that the manner in which each parent treats it comes to affect the other members of the family. Similarly, if, for example, a child is born with Down's syndrome, the manner in which each parent is affected will influence the way in which older siblings react to this new baby. When we have a normal child born to a family with an older Down's syndrome child, we have the colossal challenge of helping this child to adapt to the disabled older sibling. And, in this case, sometimes we are faced with the particularly painful difficulty of enabling the normal child not to feel guilty for being better endowed than the older sibling. Repeating myself: the parents can try to help the child, but it is definitely not totally in their hands to ensure successful adaptation to these highly complex situations.

Over the years, I have also met in my consulting-room adults who had grown up with a sibling with special needs. We must assume that those people who grew up with a disabled sibling and managed to build a satisfactory life for themselves never felt it necessary to seek professional help. However, some of these patients who came to see me told painful stories of having had to fend for themselves while watching parents devoting themselves to the disabled child. Virtually each one of these patients had created a façade of devotion and helpfulness to parents and sibling, and this supposed early self-sufficiency, "maturity", made them suspect their capacity for being genuinely loving as adults. Many of them were able to recognize their resentment for having their needs and abilities taken for granted by the parents. Further work came to show that this resentment against the parents turned out to cover up a more sensitive area, where these "normal" or even gifted people harboured an intense sense of guilt for being better equipped to achieve success in life. This sense of being "the lucky one" at another sibling's expense made it difficult, if not impossible, for them to enjoy the fruits of their own abilities.

Do parents have favourites? Why? Is this fair?

It is extraordinarily rare to find someone saying: "I *am* (or was) my parents' favourite child." This is a comment always made about another child—and even more rarely confirmed by the child concerned or by the parent "incriminated". And then, again, we would have to look far and wide before finding a parent who admitted which child is his or her favourite one. Occasionally, a parent will voice things like "I manage to talk to (. . .) more easily than to the other children" or some such phrase, but this is supposed to be a statement unrelated to the question of love.

Curiously enough, several cultures do elect "favourite" children. In parts of the world, some communities look down on the birth of a daughter while welcoming a son, and women are generally considered inferior to males. Many societies give specially favoured treatment and rights to a first-born son, and monarchies also put the first-born child in a special position. Jealousies must be expected, and perhaps having the cultural blessing for this kind of discrimination allows the parents to off-load responsibility for any decision that is resented by the other children.

My inclination was to put forward a very brief answer to this question: "Given what human nature is, it is obviously inevitable that parents should have favourites." We all value a smile, we all love someone who makes us feel good and wanted, we all resent those who time and again expose us to conflict and unhappiness. So it cannot but happen in every family that each member elects his favourite. And parents will do the same, however much they will go on claiming "I have no favourites—to me, all children are the same, they are equally loved and treated just the same as each of the others." But the moment you ask the children how true this is, they will promptly name the "real favourite" of that parent.

We do, however, have a different scenario when a child has a serious accident or is born with or develops some illness or disability. This very often leads the parents—especially, often, the mother—to form an overprotective attachment to that child. An outsider can recognize this as a response to the threat of losing that child, but what is so puzzling is the rarity of that parent reaching the point of feeling reassured or confident that there is no longer a danger of the child suffering or dying. Contrary to what happens in ordinary, non-traumatized families, here the parent feels justified in his or her exaggerated care and will always find a rationalization to explain his or her overprotectiveness. If, with normal children, the statement "he is your favourite!" leads to a denial, with children such as these, who have lived through some danger, we will most probably get an explanation to justify the special behaviour. In the medical world, something similar can be found with so-called "special patients". All sorts of out-of-the-ordinary things are implemented for the care of these patients, some of which are not always beneficial to the patient. Instead of being their usual competent professional self, suddenly the doctors are self-conscious and striving, concerned not to do something wrong—and it is well known that anyone who feels self-conscious is not functioning at his best. In the case of "special children", we can end up with very dependent individuals, usually operating well below their true potential, displaying a very subtle sense of insecurity or incompetence. With some, while the child can usually face the world in a reasonably normal way, the moment he approaches the "protective" parent he will display behaviour that brings out that parent's special ministrations, as if unconsciously the child had a sense that this parent expects this of him.

This is, obviously, not the typical "having a favourite child" scenario, and the main difference is that siblings of a child who has undergone serious surgery or developed an illness like epilepsy or diabetes struggle with considerable difficulties, as discussed earlier. If at one level they feel jealous of all the extra love the parents give that child, they also feel the urge to protect the disabled sibling, and this ends up making them feel guilty for the resentment they feel against the parent(s) who repeatedly "ignore" them. These "normal children" learn very early not to "cause more problems" for their parents. They tend to develop a sense of self-sufficiency that owes much to the parents taking these siblings' normality and competence for granted. If they achieve success in their studies and work, they often find themselves struggling with a sense of emptiness, of a void that they cannot understand or eliminate. Seeing some patients in this position, I found that they harbour (in their unconscious!) two main feelings: first, they miss that specific kind of being looked after and made to feel wanted/loved that the parents could not give them; second, they have a powerful sense of guilt for having been "luckier" than their sick sibling. Of course this is not rational, but it is the same pattern that has come to be called the "survivor's syndrome" in a totally different context. They see themselves as the lucky ones who escaped, but then feel baffled for having been spared, and they become unable to enjoy their abilities to the full.

I have gone a long way from the original question about favourites and fairness. I guess the only answer lies in our being aware of what is happening and trying not to ignore their feelings. It is not just a question of "which child you favour" but, rather, of taking an interest in how each of them feels. Whatever your feelings towards each child, it is worth remembering that each one of them will develop his own idea of where he and the others stand in the eyes of each parent. I suppose that once we are able to bear in mind how each child feels, there is a possibility that they will come to feel equally valued and, perhaps, even equally loved.

My child finds it difficult to make friends: can I do anything about this?

Every child who has difficulty in making friends is suffering from a powerful sense of low self-esteem. This is always a result of other, more complex, factors, but it is the main element that needs to be addressed. Once a child (or an adult, for that matter!) forms an image of himself as a person whom nobody wants to accept as a friend, this becomes self-perpetuating. Most people are familiar with Groucho Marx's famous dictum: "I don't want to be a member of a club that wants me for a member!" I always interpreted this as a sign of Jewish pride: blackballed by clubs by virtue of his Jewishness, Marx refused offers of membership from other clubs as these offers might be disguising some underlying anti-Semitism. Not so long ago, I realized that this same formula could explain someone's inability to make friends. Once a person (of whatever age) thinks of himself as unworthy or undesirable, then as soon as someone tries to prove him wrong, he assumes that they must be pretending not to see him for what he is.

There is a once commonly used expression that has recently gone out of fashion: inferiority complex. This emotional problem still exists, and it is as powerful as it ever was. Making friends, playing with peers, demands social-izing and being exposed to other children's likes and dislikes. When a child who is quite confident about his capacity to make friends meets another child who suggests some activity that poses dangers or creates unpleasant-ness, the former may decide with total certainty that this is a friendship he does not desire and simply turn his back and move away. When, however, this happens to a child who is lacking in confidence, he is likely to move away because of increased anxiety that he is not equipped to cope with the company of other children.

Unfortunately, self-confidence cannot be given to anyone; it has to be acquired by the child himself. One way of helping a child to achieve this is to find some local activity—music classes, dance, acting, languages, gymnas-tics, scouts, a club—where the child can both achieve some expertise that increases his self-confidence and also mix with other children who may be more welcoming of him. There is no harm in briefing the teacher or whoever runs the activity about the child's shyness and social difficulty. If this teacher or instructor does not react sympathetically, it is a sign that you are better off seeking participation in some other place.

I want to formulate this present question in a rather different way. Playing in the local playground, as much as attending a school, represents steps away from the child's emotional anchor: his home and family. There are times when the protest "I can't go there! Nobody wants to be my friend!" is a formula linked to an underlying unconscious thought that the child's absence from home causes distress to one or both parents. Quite often we hear a parent describe taking his child to nursery school and comment with barely disguised distress that "he went in and never so much as looked back!" This highlights a central conflict where parent and child are strug-gling with a desire to cling to each other, even while trying to enable each other to cope with the separation between them. If the child has managed to obtain sufficient emotional distance from the parent, he will move on, and the parent will probably adjust to this developmental step forward as a means to success in the long-term perspective. If, instead, the child is experiencing "separation anxiety"—that is, a fear of being abandoned by the parent—he will soon break down and find his way back home. This is a major challenge for the parent, who has to decide whether to "protect" the child—that is, let him stay at home—or to "be tough" by insisting that he has to go back to school (or party, playground, etc.). This configuration is very commonly found in cases of school phobia. In these specific cases, it is important to look very closely at the child's abilities, since sometimes the fear of staying at school is accompanied by other factors that may need attention in their own right. For example, the child may feel hampered by a learning disability that interferes with his self-confidence, or he may be afraid of other children who are tormenting or bullying him.

Regarding the parental side of the equation, only you can scrutinize your own feelings and decide how "ready" you are to let your child move away from you. I want to stress the fact that your child has powerful antennae and may misinterpret reactions that you may not even be aware of. Once the child experiences a fear of being deprived of his parents' love or a fear of damage to a parent, the attempt to discover how it originated becomes an academic problem. Perhaps the child had misbehaved, a parent punished him, and he took this as a sign of "worse to come". Alternatively, the parent may have happened to be upset by something precisely at the moment when the child looked at the parent, and he formed the idea that the parent was in great need of help and company. Perhaps the child witnessed some confrontation between you and your spouse and decided he should keep you company to comfort and protect you. You will probably have forgotten about these incidents, and it may not occur to you that the child's "I don't want to go there because the children don't want to play with me" might be his way of testing out whether you want him to leave or, instead, to stay with you. Quite often, these children are called "manipulators" and are said to be "striving for attention" and so forth. I feel this labelling only reinforces the child's sense that there is something wrong, condemnable, in him. Furthermore, it closes the door to what might be an effective way of eliminating the problem. If you consider the child's clinging or his "nobody wants me for a friend" as possibly being a different variation on the theme of moving away from the parents, you may be able to discuss the situation with the child. Equally important, you may have an opportunity for self-analysis and question how "ready" you are to cope with your child's leaving and with the consequent position of being left without him.

Children who have suffered accidents or illnesses will quite often present this picture of "isolation" and "being ignored". On the one hand, they may feel damaged and ill equipped to cope with the "normal children"—but, at the same time, the parents may also be terrified that some new accident or illness may befall their child. The stage is set for a closing down of horizons where a mutually reinforcing set of messages perpetuates the child's complaints. Only a careful second look, taking stock of the prevailing feelings and attitudes, can hope to establish the true importance of each of these possible factors.

My child is being bullied:
how can I help him?

I can tell a true story about this. A 10-year-old boy asked me for help over precisely this same question. I told him that a bully only tormented those children who reacted with pain and/or fear and that if the boy who kept attacking him were a typical bully, he would be disarmed by some reaction that did not suit his needs. I suggested a formula like "come on, must you carry on like this? Why can't we be friends, instead?" He changed the words, but used this strategy—and it worked.

The point of this story is that, whatever other factors are involved in these situations, the main objective must be helping your child to defend himself. Of course, school or other authorities have to be alerted to what is going on, since it is up to them to make sure that all children in the community can share its life within reasonable parameters of safety. However, your main efforts have to be directed at your child: we all live in quite an aggressive world, and it is important to equip every child to cope with its challenges.

In many cases, bullied children find it extremely difficult to be frank and candid about the circumstances of their being bullied. Some children will be afraid of incurring further punishment from the bully if he discovers who "told on him". Other children can, paradoxically, feel some unconscious compulsion to protect their tormentor. The majority of bullied children also have to contend with feelings of failure and weakness, particularly if already warned by their parents that they must show themselves to be strong. The most difficult cases will always be those children who do not trust themselves to stand up against an opponent and, instead, see one or both parents as their all-powerful protector—these children may have to contend with an unconscious idea that the parent(s) relish their role of protectors. Such a thought compels the child to continue to act helpless and in need of the parent(s)' ministrations.

There are a few short cuts that may help your child to learn to defend himself. Some parents get their child to practise boxing, judo, or other self-defence technique, and this can only be useful. When the bullying is an exceptional occurrence, perhaps demanding the intervention of some authority and the punishment of the bully will suffice. But if the bullying recurs, then a very careful probing of the child's experience of the situation is called for. This is not very easy for most parents to accomplish, but it is always worth trying it. Changing schools or moving to another area may well bring the crisis to an end, but I do believe it is important to discover whether this repeated bullying is not a pointer to your child's feeling incapable of protecting himself. At the cost of sounding terribly trivial, the question has to be asked: "Why can't your child keep out of the way of the bully?" Indeed, there are circumstances where this is totally impossible (the maltreatment of those who join some university or military unit is a common example), but it is still a point worth exploring. If you can establish that your child's complaints represent his way of indicating his helplessness, then you must consider how to help him, and the best way of doing this will vary from child to child. As mentioned, some children may benefit from self-defence classes, but others may be better served by some psychotherapy—there is, certainly, no harm in considering both avenues.

A final comment: if your family ethos considers physical aggression an offence, if not a sin, a child of yours may find it very difficult to use any part of his body as his instrument of self-defence. If, however, one parent has no trouble in hitting out physically when offended whereas the spouse condemns this use of muscular power, you may find the child hesitating over which example to follow.

Perhaps it is worth mentioning that when your child reports to you that he is being bullied, there is a fair chance that he does this at the end of quite a long struggle with his sense of pride and self-esteem. You should try very hard to find that elusive balance between being protective and yet avoiding words that may increase the child's sense of weakness. Hopefully, you will be familiar with your child's response to your attempts to comfort him, but being bullied may be his first experience of how nasty some other children can be. Comforting a child in pain, whatever its origin, always carries that element of reassuring him that the parent has not "disowned" him, that he remains the parents' "baby". Once bullies appear on the scene, the child may feel very shocked that his "baby-world" has not prepared him to cope with such creatures. In this scenario, your words of comfort and support should aim at helping the child to achieve the self-sufficiency that is escaping him: this is why simply removing the child to another school may be a counterproductive step.

My child has been accused of bullying: what should I do?

"Bullying" signifies causing distress, discomfort, or pain in order to obtain some particular advantage. It is not easy to establish that a particular bully is, in fact, not just after obtaining gains, but also seeking gratification from seeing the other child (or adult) crumple in pain. However significant this element is, it would be extremely difficult for you, as parent, to identify it. There may be times when your son repeatedly torments his younger sister and reduces her to tears. Do remember that your angry reaction to this still doesn't allow us to classify the boy's behaviour as similar to the bullies operating in schools or in society.

One more clarification: bullying usually implies physical force, actual or threatened. But what would you say about a child who forces another child to do his homework? And the child who steals his colleagues' sandwich or pocket money? The common denominator is taking advantage of another child—but would you consider them all as part of the same pattern? For the sake of our discussion, I will leave aside these various possibilities (personally, I do see them as containing the same ingredients) and simply focus on "bullying" without further qualification. I am sure that you had in mind the "bullying" that teachers report as taking place in the school playground.

It must have become clear from previous answers that I find it very difficult to accept that a particular trait is innate in the child until all possibilities have been explored about a possible environmental factor having taught the child to behave in that way. If your child is accused of bullying, the first thing I recommend is that you consider what happens in your home environment. If your child has long been known as a tormentor of his siblings, then the accusation from school may probably be well grounded. If, instead, the bullying is totally out of character with your view of the child, you should demand a careful investigation of the circumstances involving the bullying.

If you establish that the accusation is unwarranted, the problem facing you involves whoever put forward the accusation. If, however, you discover that your child has developed the habit of tormenting or abusing one or more other children, you have a complex task ahead. It is easy enough to say that you must find that kind of threat or enticement that will manage to curb your son's objectionable behaviour. But this summary procedure, however effective, still carries the danger of the boy concluding that he must be careful not to be caught next time. It is important to try to establish what prompted his treating his peers in this manner. And this may involve more skills than most parents can resort to. I would go so far as recommending that you should consult a professional for advice. Of course, if you take your son to task and he bursts out crying, confessing his sense of shame and guilt, with remorse for having hurt another child and promising never to behave like this again—congratulations. This is not a question of rewarding remorse or upholding social or religious values, but of establishing the boy's awareness of having caused pain. But this happens very rarely. Most boys in this situation will come out with a variety of rationalizations and justifications that can easily make you believe that your son has been maligned by some incompetent teacher. It is always possible that the boy may have fallen into some teacher's bad books, or he may have defended himself quite reasonably after having been attacked by one or more of his peers. The main point that a professional would try to evaluate in such situations is the child's capacity to recognize that he has hurt another child. Teachers and others will try to discover who is truly to blame for these incidents, but over and above the individual crises lies the person's capacity for concern. This is not a case of establishing whether the child feels guilty, since while feeling justified in his hostile behaviour he is unlikely to experience guilt. More important, in the long-term perspective of the child's development, is his awareness of what his behaviour caused to another person. When a child cannot perceive or acknowledge having caused pain, then there is reason to worry about the way in which he deals with his hostile feelings.

Note that I am not considering the child who, totally out of character, pinches a pen from a boy he considers privileged, nor the boy who, provoked beyond endurance, lashes out. I am focusing on a child who, repeatedly and without apparent reason or justification, hurts or humiliates another child—either with words or physically. The challenge in this case is to ascertain to what extent this boy has a personality trait that calls for professional attention or whether he is being carried along by another child or group, without knowing how to extricate himself from the situation. Each of these carries different implications, and perhaps the latter is less serious than the former. In either case, there is a good chance that your son is carrying some unconscious sense of grievance, and the manner of your reaction is liable to be interpreted as your statement of "whose side you are on". It is important to make the child feel that, whatever is happening, you are his best ally. Nevertheless, it is worth bearing in mind that some of the issues involved in bullying can often benefit from being explored in greater depth—but perhaps this should be undertaken by a professional.

THE PARENTS

4

Self-esteem, conflict, lifestyle

How does parents' self-esteem affect their relationship with their child?

Many years ago I ran a weekly group for mothers—fathers could attend, but they were always "at work", even if unemployed . . .—and children under 5 with various developmental difficulties. At one point, we had this very beautiful, blonde 3-year-old girl whose nursery-school teachers requested help because of her occasional temper tantrums. This was an intelligent child, showing very good intellectual and emotional development. She related to the other children and mothers in the group with no particular difficulty. But her mother was a very striking young woman. She was from a well-to-do middle-class family and had married a man who drank too much and never had a job. She was very articulate and quite aware of the extent to which her unhappy married life affected her repeated clashes with this child. One day I decided to confront her, and I gave her an extended list of the adjectives we had heard her throwing at her daughter: "bloody-minded", "bitchy", "manipulative", "confrontational", "obstreperous", though we had also heard her referring to the girl as "bright", "charming", "sweet", "helpful", "clever"! "How do you decide which one she is? What does it depend on?" She laughed, a wonderful, charming peal of laughter: "Simple! It all depends on how I feel at that particular moment!"

Sadly, such insight did not lead to any change in the mother's attitude towards her child. And this highlights the main problem in the present question. We all know that our feelings about ourselves will affect our perception of our position in the world, as well as our perception of the people around us. But unfortunately this process operates outside our conscious control, and in practice we only move to take stock of our words and/or behaviour if the other person reacts to us. This is easy to observe when we relate to adults, but it is usually more difficult to put under the microscope when we are dealing with our own child. Why?

A child will always believe that the parent "is right", "knows best", and similar feelings that stem from the child's fundamental position of dependence on someone he loves. In other words, in most situations the child will quickly adapt to the parent's statements and behave in a way that allows the parent to conclude that his comment, complaint, accusation, plea, injunction, or whatever had a good basis to justify it. If we say something to an adult who feels we are treating him wrongly or unfairly, he will show some (minor or major!) protest, whereas the child is more likely to comply with the parent's statement—not that the child *knows* this: such reactions are usually well outside conscious control.

From the moment a child is born, parents will deal with him in line with what *they* believe the child is experiencing. "Oh, the poor thing is hungry!" will lead to feeding, much as "he must be having some painful colic!" may lead to a consultation with the doctor. As the child grows up, each parent gradually constructs an image of that child, and this tends to coalesce into an adjective that is supposed to describe that child—bright, cheerful, stubborn, whiny, and so forth. But if we zoom in more closely, it becomes possible to observe that the point when such descriptions are put forward is not exclusively dependent on the child's behaviour: they tend to be closely linked to how *the parent* feels at that particular time.

The parent's self-esteem can impress us as being relevant during acute crises, but it can be equally relevant in a more long-term perspective. A parent who has problems with eating is almost certain to create an atmosphere where the child's feeding soon turns into an issue. The same will occur with a parent who becomes anxious when the child is out of his sight, or with a parent who dreads the presence of some physical illness. Can these examples be classified as resulting from the parent's self-esteem? In a psychology textbook, these various instances would merit a discussion to establish relevant distinctions between concepts that would best describe each one: mood, temperament, self-image, self-worth, personality traits, anxiety levels, obsessive ideas, and so on. In our present context, I suggest we can subsume them under the concept of "self-esteem"—while this is perhaps not academically correct, I believe it is quite illuminating to understand the problem under discussion.

I would like to take up another instance of "poor self-esteem". If the mother sees herself as unintelligent or cowardly or generally inferior, this will lead her to feel inadequate to care for her child. For the sake of brevity and clarity, we could assume two possibilities: she might see the child's behaviour as confirmation of her inferiority, or, alternatively, she might seek evidence in the child that she is much better than she believes, something we might call "achieving it vicariously". But the problem with both these alternatives is that, either way, the child is not being seen as *himself*. This mother is interpreting her child's behaviour in terms of what it reflects of her self-image. This raises the danger of the child gradually sensing the effect of his behaviour on the oscillations of his mother's mood, triggering an unconscious process whereby the child learns to cover up his natural abilities and way of being and, instead, creates a façade that confirms the mother's views and, hopefully, improves her self-esteem.

I regret having to complicate this picture, but this scenario can become enormously more complex when we take into account the characteristics and attitudes of the other parent. If the mother sees herself as messy and careless and the father is fussy and obsessive, the child has two models of expectations to fall in with, and the scene is firmly set for the classical accusation that the child is "taking sides", whichever choice he may make.

There is an implication in the above that a parent with good self-esteem will not have so many problems to contend with when looking after the child. Perhaps this is so, but it is not a universal truth. When his self-esteem is good enough, a father will experience less of a need to increase his sense of self-worth through his child. In other words, he does not take the child's behaviour so personally. When, however, a person feels a failure as a social being or a professional, he may attempt to use his parental role to boost his self-esteem.

Change is only possible when the parent raises the question: "Is he *really* like this?"—that is: "Am I treating him as he deserves and needs, or am I being carried away by how *I* feel about this situation?" At that point, the way may be open to consider what personal factors in the parent are influencing his approach to the child.

My partner and I often argue:
what effect will this have on our child?

My mother often quoted a saying that you yelled at the daughter, but you really meant the daughter-in-law. I always thought this a dreadfully unfair attitude, but I later recognized that it is quite a universal policy. The screamer has to get some pressure off his or her chest but presumably is still aware that a total loss of control may signify a major clash. It is this implied canniness that I so objected to, since somebody innocent is made to pay the price of being in a relationship where he or she is the weaker element.

Taking out on a child the bad feelings towards the spouse or taking advantage of a child's position of weakness to use him as a weapon against the spouse are, sadly, frequent examples of life in certain families. I must say that I believe that, in practice, the two merge into each other. Supposedly, we can "try to get the child to take sides" in the sweetest, most subtle way without biting his head off. But somehow I suspect that the effect is the same as if we had "taken out" on the child all the feelings we had stored up against our spouse. From the child's point of view, he is supposed to assume or to have assumed a position over *an issue* when in all likelihood at other times the same issue has failed to arouse the same passions that are now being thrown at him. There must be a feeling of injustice or wrong-doing, but mostly I suspect the child is simply puzzled, unable to figure out the logic of why he is under attack.

If I may quote my mother again, she often said that the main advantage of having a maid in the house was that it provided you with someone on whom you could vent your frustrations. I am sure she would never admit that she conceived me so that I could act as a buffer or a scapegoat! But one of my childhood memories has me turning to my father (I was some 7 years old) and asking him why it was that when all was going well, he referred to me as "our son", but if I had done something wrong or he was losing the argument, he would turn to my mother and say: "See what *your* son has done!!" He gave a gentle smile of embarrassment, being rather lost for words. It is quite possible that the family ethos is such that the child feels able to defend himself, rather than simply crumple into frightened silence. But turning the child into a pawn or scapegoat for marital conflicts seems to be a powerful element in the dynamics of many families. Those children I have met who were caught in these dynamics showed a façade of believing that the non-aggressive parent loved them more than the other parent did. It seems that only towards late adolescence or adulthood do these children recognize that the relationship that the doting, protecting parent maintained with the aggressive and perhaps violent parent ensured the continuation of that particular pattern. Predictably, this discovery creates considerable emotional turmoil.

On a more theoretical level, perhaps we should remember the well-known "oedipal triangle", where the child is supposed to achieve a developmental milestone when he moves from the one-to-one relationship he has (as a baby) with his mother to encompassing both parents in his world of relationships. Though postulated as a theory to explain the growing horizons of a baby's world, this differentiation operates throughout a person's life. It does seem to be the case that different people are able to have close relationships with varying numbers of persons. Some people can easily get attached to one other person but will feel completely rejected, virtually annihilated, if that person suddenly allows a third party to come close emotionally. When you have someone who is comfortably at home when one or more people join his intimate twosome, then you say they are able to have "three-body" relationships. Because of the psychoanalytic notion that adult patterns of relationship originate in the early phases of the individual's life, we hypothesize that the infant reaches a stage where he can mentally encompass both parents as a couple in his concept of the world. It is this grouping of baby relating to father and mother as two separate individuals that gave origin to the concepts of the Oedipus triangle and the three-body relationship.

Focusing on a couple who have a child, we can see that the way they will treat that child is determined by each partner's ability to see the new arrival as a welcome addition to the partnership or, alternatively, as a competitor for the love of the other partner. Perhaps this sounds theoretical and far-fetched, but we need only remember the protracted arguments couples now have when deciding whether and when to have an offspring. Clearly, all sorts of social, economic, religious, and moral arguments come into these discussions, but somewhere in each partner's conscious and unconscious mind lies the sense of security or insecurity that the arrival of a third party will bring about.

It is not rare to find couples who acknowledge the fact that a child was conceived exclusively in order to please or placate one of the partners. This is even more dramatic when this dynamic configuration involves the adoption of a child. The moment something goes wrong between the couple, the child is in danger of being attacked by the parent who resents his presence. The daily life of perfectly ordinary families contains less dramatic and, at times, even amusing situations where children are blamed for deeds or words that are beyond their ability—but they will still be attacked when a parent feels unable to address the real adversary: the other spouse.

One more word about the parent who "tries to get the child to take sides". This is clearly not an exclusive prerogative of marital life in crisis, but, rather, a common, everyday occurrence in family life. From the parents' point of view, it is part of their struggle to deal with their personal and/or marital resentments or insecurities. But it is worth remembering that, from the child's point of view, it occurs very commonly when he quotes to one or both parents some comment made by a teacher or a relative. Whatever the motivation behind quoting this comment (I can confirm that it is not always done naively and innocently!), it can sometimes give rise to sweet or tempestuous words that aim to remind the child that it is that parent's views he should adopt. I think that such a posture can only originate from a parent feeling his self-esteem challenged. The implicit or explicit demand that the child should put that parent first and follow that parent's opinions, not those of a "stranger", substantiates the notion that the parent is counting on that child's loyalty for a boost in self-esteem.

When such misuse of the child's position becomes an integral part of the family dynamics, there is, indeed, a danger that the child will fail to maintain his own, private, genuine feelings about himself and about each parent—and this can lead to a severe distortion of the child's personality. However, some children manage to keep track of what are their genuine, hidden feelings and those that family life demands they own up to. This is still one more example of a situation that can lead one child in the family to a particular type of adaptation while another child may follow an entirely different one. Development is definitely not a mathematical exercise, and we are far better at weaving explanations in retrospect than we are in predicting outcomes.

How can parents handle their conflicting ideas about bringing up children?

I am sorry: no satisfactory answer to this one! Conflict, by definition, implies that the two parties disagree, and, whatever your age and experience, you will know that when parents are able to work out compromises, this question is simply never raised. Sadly, the moment there is conflict, you have winners and losers. Nevertheless, as far as I know, whoever wins in a marital clash always has a price to pay for it, and this means that, in practice, both parties are losers.

Sometimes I think that there is a class and/or cultural element in this notion of "conflicts over child-rearing". If we think of countries where male children are valued whereas female children are often left to die, there is a general acceptance of how each child should be treated. Orthodox Jewish families are unlikely to quarrel over how boys should be prepared to carry out what is seen as male roles. Many cultures and classes take the view that the child's upbringing is the mother's domain. For a question about conflicting ideas to arise in the first place, there is an implication that both parents have equal rights over determining how the child is brought up. Is this a problem of modern, Western, middle-class, sophisticated families?

In Western middle-class families it has become extremely important to decide each precise detail of the child's upbringing. Some blame might lie with Freud discovering the extent to which early childhood experiences can influence the future development of the individual, but long before him people already argued that the child is father to the man. I believe two factors have become increasingly important over the last 150 years. One is the increasing involvement of women in the production of income to sustain the family, and the other is the (consequent?) battle of feminists and women in general claiming equal rights. Where the role of women is giving birth to children and the role of men is going out to work, there tends to be an agreement that the mothers will take charge of the children's upbringing. Those families where the wife shares in the role of earning the family money are much more likely to bring out the clashes you ask me about.

It is not just the "who makes the money" issue that is relevant in these latter families. There are many such families where there is absolute consensus over child rearing because, for example, the woman is explicitly devoted to her career and the husband is happy to take on the care of the children. The crucial point lies in each partner's definition of his or her role in the family. Over the last several decades we have come to give enormous importance to what we call "male" and "female" roles, though there is not likely to be universal agreement about what attributes go into the definition of these roles. When husband and wife disagree about how their roles should be defined, it is predictable that they will also disagree about how to influence their children so that they grow up to embody those favoured characteristics: conflict is inevitable.

It may appear that I have drifted off the main point of the question, but we must remember that the child is definitely not a blank slate or a neutral participant in this complex scenario. Each child has his own typical reaction to being caught in a situation of conflict, though to what extent this is a result of his genetic endowment and how much comes from living in a particular family is a total mystery. In practice, the moment the parents clash, there is the possibility of the child being seen to "take sides", and immediately the conflict escalates, with further, usually passionate, accusations. At this point in my clinical work I like to remind parents that, depending on the child's age, he is "taking sides" only in the parents' view of the situation. Mostly the child will have little or no understanding of the significance of the issues that divide the parents, but the younger the child, the more likely he is to "take the side" of the parent who appears the most hurt in the clash. If these situations become a repeated pattern, quite often the child will learn to keep out of the discussion. Personally, I believe that children do this switching off as they learn over the months and years that sooner or later after the storm the parents will come together again and join in whatever activities they can share. As children grow older and move on to adolescence, the possibility increases of their actually taking sides, but now with a greater awareness of the meaning of the issues being discussed.

And, I believe, it is as adolescence progresses that the *real* problems start. Now the child turns into a youngster who sets out to explore his own private definition of his gender characteristics and the many other aspects of living in society. There are repeated and often dramatic clashes between the parents as they tackle their own anxieties over what they believe the youngster is exposing himself to. I have met many parents who seek help over these situations. Some accuse the adolescent of trying to destroy not only him/herself, but also the marriage. Others want me to adjudicate which parent is preaching the correct prescriptions. Many such couples contemplate divorce, and very often other parents want support for their belief that the adolescent should leave the house, whether to be admitted to a hospital or to be taken into the care of Social Services. I try my best to find ways of helping these families with their particular problem, but there is one piece of advice that I give to each one of them: don't stop fighting, never wash your hands of the adolescent. I have found that adolescents find it almost impossible to cope with the severing of this tie. They will fight the parents individually or both together, they may quite often disappear for days or weeks—and, yet, it seems to make a difference whether the parents remain there, available and ready to forgive and fight again, or whether they refuse further contact. I do believe that adolescents experience this contact with parents as a lifeline, even if they never admit this to be the case.

Implied in the battles with adolescents is the predictable finding that very seldom will parents actually agree over how to deal with each piece of behaviour of the adolescent. There is always one critical parent and one tolerant one, one the "good, loving" parent, the other the "nasty, rejecting" one, and while they tend to swap these roles all the time, this means the adolescent can always count on (usually, only unconsciously!) having at least one of the parents available to help when the need arises.

But, as we well know, a child's adolescence is the most testing time for a marriage. This is the time when, quite often, each parent will easily—consciously, and unconsciously—see him/herself in the person of the youngster. There are constant repeated comparisons of the child's rights and duties as an adolescent with those that each parent met when they were that age. It is truly difficult for parents to be totally objective and dispassion-ate when the behaviour of an adolescent child is being debated.

The situation becomes infinitely more complex when a second marriage is involved, the simplest example being the adolescent dismissing a step-parent's view on the basis of the latter having no right to impose his or her views. A particularly complex and painful example of these marital conflicts involves the position of a step-parent who gradually discovers that his or her stepchild has become a virtual adult and who may then experience sexual feelings towards that stepchild. In the crazy, paranoid world in which we live, we now have step-parents distancing themselves from pubertal children, fearing some possible accusation or suspicion of sexual contact. And if a second husband justifies his moving away from an adolescent girl by refer-ring to the dreadful cases of men accused of molesting girls in the family, what can a mother do? She may well defend her daughter and accuse the husband of finding excuses for whatever fantasies exist in his mind, but quite often these are insurmountable anxieties, and these husbands are unlikely to change their attitude. Many conflicts of this kind can end up in the break-up of a marriage—and when this happens, the sad ritual of assigning blame ensues. No doubt everyone feels misunderstood and hurt, but I would still hope that parents in this situation manage to spare some thought for the needs of the adolescent, who tends to be the weaker link in this chain.

To state the obvious: "parental conflict over child rearing" is much easier to sort out when parents are able to engage in battle with each other and leave the child out of it.

When one parent undermines the authority of the other, what effect does this have? How can this pattern be changed?

Father forbids the child to do something, but when he goes out, mother allows it. The child is frequently in trouble at school, but mother keeps it from father. Then the teenager breaks the law—and now the mother complains that the father never disciplines him. The links between these scenarios are obvious, but can this sequence be prevented?

I like to say that life is so simple when seen in retrospect! "The wisdom of hindsight"! We are all so clever when trying to explain something that has already happened! "Of course! What could you expect? Coming from a mixed marriage!" ... "Well ... an adopted child ... what is the surprise?" ... "Got into trouble? If you knew his family, you'd understand why!" Sons of Jews, Blacks, Irish, Polish—according to one's prejudices, the explanation is easy. But if you want to make predictions, it is quite a different scenario.

In a sense, this question is a repetition or extension of previous ones. It is a specific example of what I described earlier as the common picture where parental conflict comes to be presented as revolving around a child's behaviour. Often one or both parents will claim that conflict occurs only because of the child, and the child is then accused of pitting one parent against the other. This split, where one parent is "good" (makes allowances) and the other becomes the ogre, is extremely common. Of course, sometimes the "ogre" is truly a despicable specimen, not just unfairly assigned to the role! But what the "good" parent fails to take into account is that, for the child, it is quite a mystery why, when the father (though it could equally be the mother!) is so objectionable, does the mother stick with the father? Reducing the picture in this example to its barest minimum, the child has to discover what precisely the mother expects from him. Logic will lead us to guess that the child learns to be as "good" as the mother is to him. Presumably, the child interprets the mother's "kindness" as indicating that she knows how the child feels about the father's tyrannical attitudes, hence her wish to offer the child a better deal. When the child tries to be as kind to the mother as she is to him, he may well be aiming to become the ideal companion that mother does not have in the father. Indeed, this is a pattern that is found quite commonly. However, quite often precisely the opposite development unfolds, and sons put in a position where the mother is forever covering up for the father's misdeeds form the unconscious notion that this is what the mother expects from them. In other words, they should behave like father, so that mother can continue to play the role of the forgiving, accommodating, protective partner.

The only way of changing this pattern involves both parents being prepared to work on these issues. And this is one of the most painful experiences we come across when working with children and their families: very rarely do we find parents who want to change the relationship patterns that they have developed over the years of living together. I have often found myself thinking that it can be easier to understand why some marriages break down than why and how others are held together. We meet violent, abusive spouses or some who have addictions that the other spouse professes to find unacceptable—and yet they continue living together. Is this "the power of love"? religious beliefs? unconscious, neurotic needs? the old "staying together for the sake of the children?" It does not seem to matter what justification is put forward, the fact is that the situation is acceptable to both partners—and, surely, this is all that counts. Nevertheless, as soon as a child is brought into the picture, he also deserves to be taken into account.

The kind of undermining of parental authority described in the present question emphasizes very strongly the need to elucidate what each parent sees in their child. What is the child needed for? What does the child represent for each parent?

One of the most painful episodes I found in my professional life will serve as a most unusual and disturbing example of this question of the role that a child is made to play in a marriage. I was asked to see a 10-year-old boy who attended a boarding-school. He was brought to see me at the local district hospital by the school matron. She was due to retire soon, and she wanted advice about her wish to adopt the boy. He presented no particular problems, but because of his age he was due to transfer to another school soon. As the discussion proceeded, I learnt that the boy's parents lived separately, and each of them visited the boy—occasionally. I could not quite figure out the logic of matron's plan, until eventually the relevant information surfaced: the parents did not want to divorce each other because neither of them wanted to assume full care of the boy!

A child psychiatrist is often asked to advise parents on how to help a child who is showing signs of distress. But if one finds that there are serious conflicts between the parents that make it difficult for the child to overcome his problems, it becomes virtually impossible to give effective advice. When parents are prepared to cooperate and accept professional help for the child, one can at least recommend psychotherapy. This gives the child the possibility of finding in a professional the degree of care, empathy, and warmth that is missing in the home background. All going well, the therapy can help the child to find his own "self": his own identity, apart from the influences experienced during his upbringing. In other words, if the child is identifying with one or the other parent, therapy can help him to recognize where he is taking each parent as a model (to become the same as one parent, or the opposite of the other) and, instead, discover what is his original, true self.

Is there a link, then, between those situations in childhood and behaviour in adolescence? Yes, they will always be considered as logical sequences when seen in retrospect, but this is not necessarily the case if we are focusing on a young child and trying to predict his adolescence. If that child's parents continue to treat him in that same manner, then we would have to assume that he will carry his home behaviour over to the other environments he frequents (school, clubs, jobs). There would then be a possibility of this child expecting the world to treat him as his parents had treated him. In practice, this could well mean that he would be much more easily accepted by youngsters who also have the same conscious or unconscious belief that they can get away with any kind of behaviour. We tend to call such youngsters "trouble-makers", antisocial. If our "child" gets into trouble with the police and now the mother demands that the father should act the disciplinarian, I would interpret this as her way of saying that the adolescent's current behaviour has all been the father's fault. In this case the mother is clearly unable to take responsibility for her actions, and this last step only highlights what might be seen from the beginning: this mother's "kindness" is a brand of "protectiveness" that ignores the child's need for rules and discipline.

But we must bear in mind that all of the above makes sense only if it is established that the child is normal and that his behaviour is a response to the parents' attitudes to him. A child may have a specific constitutional problem that prevents him from behaving in a manner that is acceptable to both parents. However difficult a diagnostic problem this is, it is important to establish the child's ability to respond to the parents' expectations. It is quite wrong to take it for granted that the child in the configurations we have been discussing is fully developed in an age-appropriate manner. This must always be assessed very carefully.

As for what the parents can do to change the pattern: to begin with, I tend to recommend that they go out for dinner together (couples like these seldom spend time together!), forget that they are parents, and try to converse as two adults who used to love each other. If this goes well, then they should then try to discuss their views of each other's parenting and attempt to work out a unified strategy to deal with their child. If this is not feasible, perhaps they should consider seeing a professional long-term (i.e., for their conflicts, not as part of helping the child), since in all probability the child's behaviour is touching some Achilles' heel in one or both of them. In line with this hypothesis, perhaps I should mention one of my diagnostic gambits: after I hear how each parent describes the child's behaviour and what each makes of this, I ask them: "Well, who does he take after?" I still have to find a family where a troublesome child is not seen as a replica or a renewed version of someone in an earlier generation.

Why shouldn't I disparage, belittle, or complain about my spouse (or ex-) to our child?

I think that from very a young age a child will hear a parent's words as indicating what *that* parent wishes him to learn. If one parent speaks English to the children while the other talks to them in Spanish, then most children will learn to address each parent precisely in the language they have picked up from them. I believe the same principle applies to all kinds of things children absorb from living within the family and exchanging verbal and nonverbal communications with each parent. The child picks up very easily how each parent treats the other and how each refers to the other in his or her absence. A rather trivial example: the mother insists that the child should always use a knife and fork when eating, but when she is not there, the father sometimes picks up the barbecued pork ribs with his fingers. Some children will remind father of what mother demands, others will "tell on" father to their mother—the variations are endless, but they certainly illustrate how sensitive children are to these "mixed messages".

91

In precisely the same way, the child picks up what each parent thinks of the other, and in all likelihood in the absence of one of the spouses he will voice comments about that parent that will meet with the approval of the parent who is there. All parents have had this experience, which, sadly, does not lead most of them to keep to themselves those negative views they have about their partner. So we have the question: what is wrong with this?

However beastly a parent is, somehow most young children still manage to love that parent. This is not so true for an older child, who may well come to discern those areas over which a parent can be loved, while being quite critical of unacceptable behaviour. I have always been puzzled by children of parents who often get drunk and behave in a shameful and even hurtful manner—somehow their children will always try to make excuses for this behaviour, even though they learn quite early to keep away from the drunk parent. The unfaithful husband who is kicked out by his jealous, resentful wife quite often manages to mobilize feelings of support or solidarity from some of his children. That parent who is totally incapable of saying "sorry" to his child can still be the object of warm feelings on the part of that same child. But, then, when children are very young, what choice do they have?

When the child learns that he must not voice to one parent his loving feelings for the other (disparaged) parent, at the risk of eliciting resentment and bitterness, then the result is the development of a façade: attitudes and behaviour that do not correspond to the child's true feelings. In a way, this mechanism could be seen as part of the general process of coping with ordinary life, an integral part of socialization, where we learn not to say or do things that might offend or hurt others. There is, however, an important difference between learning to be courteous and considerate and the building of (mostly unconscious) defences that can protect the child from anxiety and fear. A point can be reached where the façade, which initially began as an adaptation to a specific home situation, comes into operation in situations outside the family, and the child can experience his position in life as one where that façade becomes his "normal" external self. The theory is that what might be called his true self has become submerged within his unconscious. I must, however, stress that I am definitely not talking of hypocrisy or play-acting, but of a process of development that makes the person oblivious to this suppressed real self. These are the people who strike you as being "too good", just too unflappable, not out of a deliberate manoeuvre, like politicians, but as if this were their real, genuine, way of living in the world.

This would be one major justification for the inadvisability of berating your partner to your child. But on another level it could be argued that this berating is counter-productive because the child ends up being tempted to support the vilified victim of your bitterness. I think that from quite early on children can appreciate the roles of aggressor and victim. This certainly does not mean that their judgement will match the parent's! Supposedly, for you to berate your spouse must mean that you feel the victim of his malice or rudeness or irresponsibility or whatever: our imaginary child may well "take your side" by way of protecting you from your partner's attacks and soothing your pain. But there are dangers you must take into account: your partner may be doing precisely the same complaining about you to the child, and after some time the child may come to feel that you are getting things out of proportion and being unfair. This may gradually move him to being protective (or taking the side) of your spouse.

All considered, good sense dictates that you should refrain from making comments about your spouse's behaviour. If the child witnesses a clash, let him make of it what he can. If the child complains to you about something your spouse has done to him, do sympathize with the child, acknowledging how he must feel, but try to refrain from the obvious "don't I know it? I get the same treatment. . . ." True, such a comment may make the child feel corroborated and supported. But there is a danger that the child may feel that you have usurped some of his pain, deprived him of the sympathy he craved for, and, perhaps worse, feel guilty that he has given you ammunition to condemn your spouse—and then feel tempted to defend him or her. You must bear in mind the possibility that the child is "exaggerating" your spouse's "dreadfulness" because he has learnt that this is what you want to hear. It is a safer and wiser policy to show sympathy and concern but at the same time stress to the child that it is your spouse to whom he should be addressing his complaints.

In a marriage marked by continuous conflicts, the day is bound to arrive, as the child grows older, when he asks the dreaded question: "How can you put up with it?" This is a difficult one, because in all probability this is a question you will have asked yourself a few million times without ever managing to find a satisfactory answer. So at least try to respect your child's intelligence and, whatever you do, don't say that classical line: "I think children need parents—I wouldn't dream of inflicting a divorce on you." Instead, just assume that your child does not really expect an answer; shrug your shoulders, make some noncommittal sound—and, leave it at that.

The problem here is that most of these wonderful answers occur to us only in hindsight or when we are discussing someone else's problems. Self-control cannot be prescribed. Furthermore, whatever your temperament, however self-contained you usually are, you also have a breaking point. And the threshold for this will plunge much lower if you are or feel you are alone, unprotected. Loneliness is a most soul-destroying experience, and if your child (or children) is your only reliable company, inevitably you will sooner or later turn to him as confidante. As a psychoanalyst, perhaps I should register at this point that many people come to see me because of needing someone to speak to: not necessarily because of needing therapy, but out of a need to voice some thoughts and feelings that they have no one else to share with.

Bad relationships in families can repeat from generation to generation: how can this cycle be broken?

In truth, breaking a cycle such as this is one of the most difficult goals to achieve. Time and again, throughout my professional life, I have met people who were absolutely determined to avoid their parents' mistakes, only to find that, contrary to their scrupulous manoeuvres, they had fallen into precisely the same patterns. How can one explain this? When we pursue a goal that involves no other human being, there is a reasonable chance of attaining it. When, however, we are dealing with relationships, we have to acknowledge that "it takes two to tango"—that is, any changes in a twosome will demand that both partners are prepared to implement them.

As your question stands, a simple, honest answer to it would be for me to say that "I don't really know". Of course, I could give you all kinds of formulae, but for any of these to work, it would be necessary, first and foremost, that your partner be also willing to accept changes in the relationship. We have all met many people professing to desire changes in their relationship, and yet, in practice, this seldom leads to successful outcomes. However sad our ancestors might find this, it is still a fact that our present Western societies have come to see separation and divorce as a more convenient and easier solution to any "bad relationships" in families. In other words, "not to repeat the mistakes of our parents" while preserving the existing relationship demands serious and hard work on the part of all the people involved.

I would like to mention a few points that may help us to identify some of the subtle and diverse forces at play here.

We are exposed to those "bad relationships" from the moment we are born. As we grow up, we are forever exposed to words, customs, attitudes, habits, styles that we knowingly and unknowingly come to accept and adopt as being part of our family, our group, our community way of life. Of course, as we grow older, we discover that the way the people around us react to each other in fact indicates feelings and impulses. The process whereby we learn to distinguish between the apparent, observable behaviour and the underlying feelings that are not always so discernible is quite a puzzling one. As our horizon widens and we come to meet people outside our nearest family, we realize that people in other families treat each other in different ways. Discovering this poses a formidable problem, as it forces us to ponder the implications of this for our own lives. A child finds it very difficult to actually allow himself to recognize that the way his family lives is dysfunctional.

I suspect it is only around the age of 5 or 6 that we begin to grasp the intensity of the feelings of anger, pain, and perhaps even hatred that one or both of our parents experience and show in their ordinary behaviour. I want to emphasize how subtle and complex are the stages that a child's understanding of his world will have to go through before a word or piece of behaviour will be identified as "bad" and not the one and only way in which that parent might have expressed himself.

Consciously and unconsciously, we find ourselves taking sides. Then there are times when we find ourselves at the receiving end of the same interactions we observed as an onlooker. For example, it can happen that a mother treats her spouse with contempt and repeatedly reduces him to some pathetic state of shame and helplessness; he turns to the child and finds comfort in playing a game of chess with him. One day the child plucks up enough courage to question the mother about this, and she explains her behaviour by describing the father's repeatedly squandering money on drink and gambling without consideration for the family's needs. The child thinks about this interaction and, somehow, decides who is right and who is wrong and, presumably, forms some ideas as to how he wishes his parents would treat each other. Perhaps he also "decides" how he will behave one day when he reaches their age. Let us assume that the child tends to devote himself very responsibly to his schoolwork. But then comes the day when he fails to complete one of his homework tasks—and suddenly he finds his mother lashing out at him as if he were an exact replica of his father. How does he now assess the whole complex issue of who hurts whom and why his mother behaves in that way? Presumably, if up to that point he had found justification for his mother's way of treating his father, he may now find himself quite muddled about right and wrong attitudes. A further complication is that, at an unconscious level, he may find himself interpreting his parents' behaviours as typical of their respective genders. If we now also bring into the picture the child's contact with other children and adults, we can see how difficult it must be for him to elaborate all these experiences and form his views of the people with whom he will spend his life.

Perhaps the problem is simpler if only one of our parents is consistently cast as the villain. A son whose father is repeatedly violent may decide quite early on that he will never resort to violence, much as his sister will decide to try to avoid men who are or might become violent. But, then, often we find precisely the opposite happening: the son turns violent, and his sister chooses a violent man for a partner.

The only explanation I can offer is that these models to which the child is exposed create memory traces, the majority of which remain submerged in his unconscious. Psychoanalytic theory postulates that these experiences lead to the formation of images of self and others that affect the gradual development of the child's concept of himself as an individual and of those around him. For the observer, it is not difficult to spot those moments when the child is "behaving just like his father (or mother)", but the child very rarely perceives this himself. It is only in adolescence and adulthood that we will find ourselves regretting that we behaved in the manner we had earlier condemned in our parents—but even then this tends to occur in retrospect, seldom in time to stop us from "behaving badly".

The comments above concern an individual who finds himself repeating behaviours he had condemned in his parents; however, the question focused, instead, on the repetition of relationship patterns, and this would signify the involvement of family members who are in continuous interaction. If you, as an individual, have reached the point where you acknowledge that you are repeating the parental mistakes you wish to avoid, the first task is to discover precisely what it is that triggers off that behaviour. This is definitely not a case of trying to find someone to blame; rather, it is an attempt to identify what brings into action an Achilles' heel you may or may not be aware of possessing. You may be lucky and discover that the factor operating that trigger is irrelevant: all you need is to work on yourself to eliminate or control that weak spot in your personality. If you find that it is your new boss who provokes the unwanted reaction, you may have to change departments or find a new job. But if you establish that your reactions are an integral part of your marital living patterns, then you have to convince your partner that *both* of you have to find new ways of relating to each other. I repeat: it is pointless to discuss "who is to blame", since by the time the problem comes to your notice, any notion of what is cause and what is effect is totally irrelevant. What follows, for better or for worse, will now depend on your partner's reaction to your arguments. With luck, he or she may recognize having become caught up in an interaction that produces pain in you or, in fact, in both of you—and decide to tackle the problem. Sometimes couples can find better ways of relating on their own; if this is not the case, you should consult a marriage counsellor.

What effect does it have on the child if both parents are of the same sex?

I confess that this is strange territory for me. I have not, so far, had any experience with children being brought up by parents of the same sex. I suppose the vast majority of my colleagues are also in the same position. On the basis of what experience I do have, I would assume that this child would face many difficulties while growing up. Presumably it is easy enough to take it for granted that he will be seen as exceptional by his peers, much as any other child from an unusual background would be. But this is an easy guess. Children will always react to children they perceive as different, but given the opportunity to discover the individual child behind the descriptive label, things take a normal course. We have ample knowledge of these problems in England, where multiple minorities are seeking integration with the rest of the population. Each individual child has different capacities to cope with the inevitable clashes, but on the whole this tends to be no more than a period of integration. As we can guess, the ethos of the environment that a child joins is all-important (a sympathetic headmistress, well in control of staff and pupils, is a virtual guarantee of success), but the child's home principles are equally important as a factor determining the outcome of the process. If the parents are keen to interact with the new community, integration may be much easier for the child; if, on the other hand, the parents warn the child not to adopt the customs of the neighbourhood, this may create anxieties and conflicts of loyalty in the child. And when a child becomes self-conscious and suspicious, this tends to arouse antipathy in the other children and leads to confrontation.

These suppositions and inferences that refer to social integration are reasonably easy to make. What is infinitely more difficult is to imagine the individual emotional development of the child being brought up by parents of the same sex. Focusing on "ordinary" children, we speak of an "oedipal" phase in which the child comes to differentiate between male and female people and supposedly has strong feelings towards the main representatives of these genders—namely, his parents. We tend to quote the oedipal myth as if it had been Freud's invention, but long before him we had infinite numbers of myths and legends depicting the triad of child and parents. The very Judeo-Christian biblical story of the start of family life puts forward a male–female conjunction that produces a child. So this idea that children have parents of opposite sexes does go very far.

Over the centuries there have been endless changes in what are considered "masculine" and "feminine" attributes in each culture. The present rage in our Western world about the "equality of sexes" would cause immense surprise and amusement, if not horror as well, in many other cultures—not only past, but many present ones as well. Each one of us has a gallery of what we consider typical traits of each gender, and individuals will always be judged in line with the prevailing preconceptions of each environment they visit or move into. In terms of our present question, the one and only element of this whole complex pattern that concerns us is the issue of what leads a child of a particular gender to develop those characteristics that that society associates with that gender. This question is so difficult to answer not just because of the danger of coming across as ignorant or prejudiced, but the related fact that it is not easy to establish what precisely makes a boy develop masculine traits and a girl feminine ones. The obvious all-embracing answer is to say that this development will depend on the attributes of the child's constitutional endowment (anatomical make-up, glands, hormones) as influenced (modified, added to, suppressed) by the environment (parents, wider family, community) in which the child grows up. The trouble with this definition, in spite of its indisputable good sense, is that when our task is to assess how one specific individual child is being affected by his parents, it represents no more than a very broad baseline.

Many people defend the rights of two adults of the same sex to have or to adopt a child, much as others condemn it as despicable or selfish. But I have restricted myself to that element of the question where we wonder about the child involved. Whatever our views about the adults, we simply cannot guess how an individual child will develop. To take other examples: should we have allowed adults deformed by Thalidomide to have children?

We have families where children of one sex will almost certainly develop particular illnesses: should we agree that foetuses of that sex should be aborted? Such examples are, in fact, valid only in terms of the responsibility that parents hold towards the children they produce, but they say nothing about the actual development of a child born to such parents. At the end of the day, we have to wait and discover what these children brought up by parents of the same sex will say about their childhood and their view of the world in which they grow up.

I am sure that some research will be conducted on this issue, and I will be particularly interested in learning how *each child* felt about his upbringing over the course of his first twenty or so years.

5

I'm in an egocentric whirl of self-recrimination about how I treat my child: how can I break out of this and focus on my child again?

The answer to your question lies in your wonderful image of the "egocentric whirl of self-recrimination". This suggests an awareness that the blame being thrown at yourself is the end product of a multitude of emotional experiences that become too enmeshed and, therefore, virtually indistinguishable. If we could focus a powerful lens on this maelstrom and identify the emotions that bring about that sense of self-recrimination, perhaps you might find it easier to decide which way to move—if not right then, at least the next time the situation threatens to overpower you.

Let us focus on two examples: not managing to soothe a crying infant, and not coping with a toddler's stubbornness. Soothing your crying infant seems a million years away from trying to manage your toddler's stubbornness, but they are examples of situations that can so easily bring about that same self-recrimination. With the infant, you are bound to make gigantic allowances to explain the crying, since mothers will not attribute ulterior motives to the infant, because the "poor things" can hardly think and recognize the world in which he lives. With the toddler, all becomes infinitely more complicated. You will have come to consider him a more "mature" child, quite capable of being obedient and sensible, so whenever he chooses to be stubborn, words like "manipulating", "trying to get attention", "getting at me" become much more common. In spite of these differences, I put the two examples together because in your scenario you depicted yourself as being the one in charge of the child, and therefore the one and only person expected to deal with the situation.

We should try to isolate each step in the process under discussion. In real life this is virtually impossible, since events just tend to cascade around you, and you become quite incapable of taking stock to see what precisely leads to what. Your description is very clear: the infant cries, the toddler disobeys, and each is then facing a parent who, starting from ordinary good will and a determination to help, gradually finds him/herself inside that "whirl of self-recrimination" where guilt, shame, resentment, helplessness are quite overwhelming.

As the sequence begins—the infant crying, the toddler disobeying—you leave aside whatever it was you had been dealing with, and you turn your attention to the child. Presumably, you take in that the child is announcing that he can no longer keep to himself and is expressing an audible message that some outside input is desired, if not expected. You are likely to take that in, but depending on what you had been doing, you may wish to bargain for a moment of tolerance. In fact, you may even hope that the crying or disobedience will abate and you won't have to deal with it urgently. Such a lot depends on what you were previously doing!

Let us assume that you were doing something that can wait and that this time you can turn to your child without an immediate sense of being inconvenienced. You will cuddle your baby or try to reason with your toddler. If this doesn't work, you are likely to feel puzzled, and, with luck, you will try some alternative way of pacifying your child. If this fails, there is a good chance that some frustration will surface from within you, and if there is disappointment, there is also a sense of annoyance that can grow very quickly into impatience and anger. Of course you know full well that this change in your mood is likely to affect your child, but such knowledge seldom allows you to regain control of your emotions. This is the point of maximal danger. From your initial wish to help, you have moved to a sense of impotence and failure, and the danger here is your perceiving your child as responsible for making you experience such painful feelings. How can one measure the gradations between being angry with your child and that intense feeling of passion that is sometimes called hatred?

The relevance of these nuances is that very different kinds of reactions correspond to each of them. If you do subsequently find that the baby responds to a new attempt by you to soothe him, your sense of failure is compensated for by the relief of finding him at peace again, plus the extra reward of having discovered how to help him. But the opposite extreme—when you just wish you could leave the room or the house because you are frightened you might "do something to the baby" (yelling, shaking, hitting, or worse!)—leads to a sense of failure that is magnified by the guilt of having harboured such feelings towards your own child. However much you blame the baby or the toddler, you are likely to feel horrified at discovering that you could actually hate your own child.

It is not difficult to describe all these emotions, and I am sure you have recognized these various stages in your feelings. You mentioned the "self-recrimination" you experience, and this will hit you whatever the stage to which the above sequence has progressed. However, if your baby or toddler "gives in" and is comforted without too much effort, any sense of guilt will be compensated for by the knowledge that your initial "failure" led to an effective intervention. If, on the other hand, your baby or toddler continues to cry or disobey in spite of all your efforts to help him, then the sense of guilt will contain a much more painful dimension of self-blame. Here, you are not only feeling hostile to your unresponsive child, but you have to deal with the discovery of feelings and impulses in your self with which you may be quite unfamiliar. At this point, it becomes plainly impossible for you to attend to the child's needs because you are now afraid of your own self.

How can you short-circuit this sequence? The one and only rule I can name is to think at all times that the child is experiencing something he can only express in the way he has shown. Your response is totally dependent on how you interpret his crying or stubborn behaviour. If this does not work, you have to assume that he knows no other way of expressing himself. The only way of avoiding an escalation of the situation after you first attempt has failed is to ask yourself: "If this isn't what he wants, then *what else* can it be?" In other words, you have to find a different interpretation for his behaviour. With the baby, you have to accept that he lacks the words to convey his precise needs, and you have to try various solutions, until you discover what he has sought to obtain. With the toddler, you can only try something like: "I really can't imagine what you are driving at—what is it you want?" Of course, the way you formulate your questions will depend on his age and personality, but your only chance of avoiding that sense of guilt and failure is to consider that he is struggling with something he cannot solve on his own. Rather than taking your toddler's stubbornness as an attempt to break you down, it is best to show a sympathetic face and get across the message that you are not hurt or angry and that you are quite convinced that you know where you stand. In other words, the crying or the stubbornness should be seen as signs of distress, rather than challenges personally directed at you.

All toddlers will put you to the test at one point or another, but as long as you show that you are in control of yourself and the situation, they are bound to "give in" and fall in with your demands or rules or expectations. At the risk of sounding most improbable and terribly soppy, your toddler's performance should be interpreted as his saying something like: "How can you do this to me! It can only be because you don't love me! And I hate you if you don't love me! Please show me that you still love me!" In other words, if the clash started over issues like water spilled on the carpet or the refusal to put on a shirt, the emotionality that unfolds no longer has any connection with the practical issue but with the child's most elemental requirement for personal security: parental love.

The moment you lose control of your emotions, most toddlers will experience panic because they no longer see you as a source of help and security, and this is a feeling they cannot cope with. Insecurity is bound to lead them to escalate the behaviour you see as a provocation, until you explode and, in some families, even hit them. Paradoxically, whether they cry or not, they will react with relief—not because "they have won", but because they believe you have regained control of your feelings (i.e., instead of distressed and unhappy, you are now only angry), and they can feel safe again.

In summary, my "mantra" would be that, if you fail to soothe your baby or win over your toddler, you should try to find some different way of interpreting your child's behaviour. The moment you take his distress personally and feel that he is "showing you up", you are lost. This sense of being attacked is very difficult to overcome and tends to be not only self-perpetuating, but also self-fulfilling, because it makes the child feel insecure.

It is normal for parents to feel guilty when their child has a disability: how does this guilt affect the child?

I am sure that by "normal" you mean something like common, usual, inevitable. As long as you do not mean "logical", I can entirely agree with you. I am stressing this difference because "disability" encompasses far too many things, and it is important to try to define what precisely the child's disability is and what possible role the parent(s) might have had in this. And yet even when we unravel all relevant data and can reach a clear *cause* for the disability and prove that there is no parental role in this, there is no guarantee that this will assuage any guilty feelings the parent(s) may harbour.

I can hear myself waffling away but not really producing a clear answer to the question. In a sense, it is not easy to establish a clear correlation, a cause–effect formula, to link the parents' feelings and how they affect the disabled child. We can have a parent totally consumed by guilt who is forever overzealous about protecting the child, and the child, for his part, feels enormously loved and cared for, whereas another child in the same position may resent "being babied" or "being treated like a ninny". But how will we determine whether either reaction is dependent on the child's disability or, in fact, on his personality?

We also have to consider that feelings of guilt are not the only ones that a child's disability can arouse in the parents. I remember a child with cerebral palsy whose mother performed all expected duties, but who harboured a powerful resentment against her child. The mother was in her early forties, and the father had children from a previous marriage. This child was conceived amid considerable ambivalence, and when his disability became clear, the mother felt enormously betrayed and bitterly resented the life-long commitment ahead of her. In this case, both parents struggled with very complex emotions, but guilt was mostly apparent in the father, who felt unable to influence his wife's feelings. I also knew a boy who had a nearly fatal fall in ghastly circumstances that shocked his parents more than it seemed to shock him. He seemed to show no after-effects from the accident, but his mother went on to pamper and make allowances for him for many years. Was she moved by guilt? Probably, but equally or even more important, she was affected by the awareness that a child she had given up for dead had remained alive and healthy. What makes these cases so difficult to evaluate is that there are so many complex and subtle factors influencing the parents' feelings about their disabled child.

Consider a couple in their late thirties who are told that the baby the mother is carrying has been found to have Down's syndrome. Many parents in this situation decide to carry the pregnancy to term, and it is a painful fact that very often the world will assume that the parents feel guilt or remorse or resentment or hostility towards their disabled child, whether the parents confirm this or deny it. One of the biggest problems with disability is the complex web of prejudices it arouses in each of us. If I had a disabled child, I am sure that I would feel hugely ashamed if I found that my fatherly love was in some way mixed with guilt and pity. But just to show how complex this subject is, let me mention a friend whose daughter required glasses from a very early age. This was only discovered thanks to the mother's sensitive assessment of how the child dealt with objects around her. Surprising as it may seem, this mother felt guilty about her child's defective vision! Should "needing corrective lenses" rate as a *disability*? These are not issues to argue over: parental guilt can be present even with a normal child, and, on the whole, it is not taken into account when assessing the child's reaction to the way he was brought up. But once there is disability present, it always raises this issue of how the child's development is affected by the parents' feelings over the disability. I am trying to emphasize how difficult it is to focus on a specific aspect of the child's emotional life and establish whether this results from his psychological constitutional endowment, from his disability, or from the parental input.

As a professional looking at a disabled child, more than with the ordinary kind of child, I must be careful to evaluate *that* individual child and his family, however much I am bound to be influenced by knowledge of other cases. At this point, I am considering not how the parents' feelings affect the child but, rather, the parents' anxiety to know the significance of whichever disability has been diagnosed, in terms of the prognosis for the child's future development. Our knowledge of many types of disability is still relatively poor, but these last few decades have brought major discoveries regarding the causes of many disabilities, and this is, in fact, one of the most exciting fields in medicine and particularly paediatrics.

How children are affected by their parents' feelings takes us into the field of psychology, and regrettably most of our findings are dependent on the knowledge and experience of who makes the assessment—so often, two professionals seeing the same child may come up with two different views. Some children with physical disabilities blame their parents for their disability, much as others with the same disability will acknowledge the parents' efforts to counterbalance their deficiency, and others still who hold no one responsible for their disability even though they may complain about the way their parents treat them. One thing is certain: the moment a parent feels *guilt* for any wrong he finds in his child, he will be influenced by this sentiment in his approach to the child. He will be watching the child, always expecting to find elements that will confirm the reason for the guilt or, contrariwise, assuage it, if only temporarily. And this is where you find danger, because if the child has normal capacities to assess the sentiments of those around him, he will have to make sense of the parent(s)' way of approaching him. My guess is that if the child senses the parent's guilt, he may find himself trying to comfort that parent. I suspect that unconsciously this child will then feel that his own feelings about his disability are being ignored and the parental guilt has taken the place of greatest importance.

If I may give an example: all children have minor accidents. At one extreme, we can hypothesize parents who are forever shouting at the child, calling him clumsy, inattentive, destructive, provocative, and so forth. Whether the child is normal or not, gradually these adjectives are bound to coalesce into the child's self-image. At the other extreme, let us imagine a child who is born with a fragility of blood vessels and a tendency to haemorrhage. There is a good probability that the child's concept of the seriousness of his condition will be highly dependent on the degree of protectiveness the parents display towards him. That first "clumsy" child may, at some point, be found to have visual deficits. It is almost certain that his parents will feel guilty for not having spotted this earlier, but how can we predict how their resultant attitudes (trying to make up for their "failure") will affect the child's self-image? As for the second child, he may develop into a phobic, frightened person, much as he may become some dare-devil, forever testing out the supposed shortcomings of his body: how can we establish the correlation between such developments and the parents' initial efforts at protecting the child from dangerous traumas?

To some extent, all these speculations are flawed. They are explanatory constructs, where I am trying to make sense of the problem raised in this question. If at all possible, in such a painful situation as having a disabled child, it is best to resort to logical thinking and ordinary good sense. The ideal is for parents to scrutinize their feelings and try to work on them—not "for the good of the child", but to try to make their lives more tolerable. Feeling guilt towards a child is probably one of the most soul-destroying emotions, and it can only vitiate the parents' approach to that child. If they manage to reach some kind of "exculpation" or a more balanced view of their responsibilities, there is bound to be a positive change in their approach to that child. I believe that, by definition, children feel responsible for all pain their parents suffer, and if instead of a guilty, mortified parent they observe a self-confident one, they are more likely not to feel the need to protect or to make up to that parent.

Why do parents blame or label their child when he is ill, misbehaves, or fails, rather than dealing with what he is trying to convey?

This question contains an important statement: that the child in question is "trying to convey" something. I happen to believe that our words, actions, feelings are the result of a complex mixture of conscious and unconscious elements. This implies that the overt expression of our thoughts and feelings may well contain meanings that are not easily discernible by those around us—in fact, they may even be unknown to us! This being so, when "the child is sick, misbehaves, fails" it is possible to assume that the child is trying to *convey* something that is not quite what the parent (or other outsider) perceives as "sickness, misbehaviour, or failure". However, such an assumption is still not proof that the child had any such intention.

This point is well illustrated by a classic Jewish-mother joke: a son doesn't finish the chicken soup his mother serves him, and she asks him: "What's the matter? Don't you love me any more?" The mother assumes that the son is conveying negative feelings towards her by leaving the soup on his plate: but would he ever agree that this is so? Perhaps a more serious example can be found with preverbal babies: how can a mother know what her baby is experiencing? Obviously, she has no other option than to follow whatever her knowledge (plus intuition!) tells her. And here we can see a very interesting dividing line. On the one hand, we have mothers who will implement one "solution" (feeding, changing nappies, moving the child to another position, etc.) in the absolute conviction that *they know* what the child wants/needs; on the other hand, we find mothers who will *try* a succession of measures, searching for the one that will bring comfort to the baby.

I believe this can be transposed to the scenario of older children. When an older child is sick, misbehaves, or "fails", he may, indeed, have an unconscious need/wish to *convey* some particular feeling to us—but we must always maintain an element of doubt regarding each interpretation we reach about that behaviour of the child. His tummy-ache may be an expression of a fear that his parents' latest argument might lead to a divorce, but then again it might indicate some acute digestive condition. When the child spills ink or paint on his schoolbook, this may relate to an underlying anxiety over the reaction of a new teacher, but it may also be an early sign of a fever or, in fact, no more than an accident. When a child does not manage to read the books his single parent gives him, this may well indicate his resentment at a recent divorce, but it may also result from an unrecognized dyslexia.

In brief, from the child's point of view, it is most important to consider the possibility of some non-psychological element in his behaviour, words, or appearance, before we conclude that there is "a message" there. Of course, such a message may well be superimposed on an underlying physical component, and the challenge is to disentangle which belongs where.

But the question really focuses on the parents. What is the advantage of "blaming the child"? Why do they need to label a child? I think this has to do with our low tolerance of uncertainty. We all hate "not to know"; we find it difficult to tolerate any gaps in our picture of the world. We have an unconscious compulsion to form clear pictures that will help us, guide us, in how to proceed. This is, predictably, much more pressing when we are involved in a relationship of dependence, where we are responsible for another human being. It is easy, therefore, to understand that when we have a parent who feels totally responsible for a child's welfare, there will be a temptation to jump at certainties: and, in a way, each label signifies an assessment, an explanation, of what the parent has to deal with. Blaming the child tends to serve the same purpose: when something is seen as the child's fault, there is no longer any need to worry whether that something is a sign of another, more serious problem that may follow. Usually, this satisfies the parent and life can go on. But there are times when this can create a serious problem, when the child accepts the blame or the label as "the correct" significance of his original behaviour. This, I believe, is how we come to find innumerable families where, for example, a child does not attend school because of his tummy-aches, which require the mother to take him to the doctor in case there is something behind his complaints. As far-fetched as it might sound, I do think that there is a first time when the child does have some digestive trouble that causes him pain and makes his mother feel very anxious and insecure; the visit to the doctor's surgery then brings relief and peace to both child and mother. If there follows a situation where some anxiety of the child's produces discomfort or malaise and he holds his tummy or runs to the toilet and the mother responds by "diagnosing" a digestive problems that calls for a visit to the doctor, we may have a pattern coming into being.

These are the cases where your words come to life: if only that parent tried to discover what anxieties the child is struggling with, perhaps the pattern might be broken. However, this can only happen if the parent is able to tolerate the hard work of trying to "fish out", to help the child find the words that might elucidate what precisely are the fears from which he would like someone to relieve him. Not easy: not because the child is stubborn or contrary, but because very often the child himself is not really aware of what is upsetting him. From his point of view, it is a pain he experiences or a failure he feels humiliated by, or whatever thoughts or feelings he found his psyche expressing through his body.

Difficult work—but, as I have said earlier, a goal well worth pursuing.

How do you apologize to a child when you are in the wrong? And what if your spouse is in the wrong and refuses to apologize?

The first part of the question is so simple that I fail to understand the reason for the question: the moment you realize you were wrong, you approach the child and say *"Sorry"*. Depending on the child's age, do explain how you consider you were wrong, but on the whole I think you needn't embark on any detailed explanation of what you believe made you go wrong. There is always the danger of your overshooting what is required, and it is best to make an apology and leave it at that. If you allow your feelings to push you into detailed explanations as to what was happening to you and led to your being unfair to the child, etc. etc., you run the risk of making the child feel obliged to do something to soothe your feelings. This means that from finding himself badly treated and perhaps experiencing some resentment against you, suddenly the child finds himself feeling guilty and called upon to give you some solace for the distress implied in your explanation. Indeed, the worst scenario is if, when explaining why you did or said something wrong, you mention that the child had done something that threw you off balance. Now the child cannot but feel that the whole incident was his fault . . . and so, the "sorry" becomes no more than a "*j'accuse*" indictment.

The second half of the question belongs to the issue of parents disagreeing over the handling of the child. To avoid any doubts, let me say that I see no difference here whether the spouses are together or divorced, married or not. I believe the issues are still the same, even though it might be argued that some legal prescriptions apply and are not being respected. This is true and valid, but if our concern is with the child, then legal technicalities are not relevant, whether we focus on the parent who has custody of the child or the one who doesn't.

I believe there is a significant difference between whether the child tells you of some wrong your spouse committed or whether this actually takes place in your presence. From the child's point of view, it is part of his growing up that he has to build a picture of each parent, and this involves taking on board how each parent treats the other. If the child experiences the parents along the lines of "he loves me"/"he loves me not", he is bound to give a negative mark to the parent who wrongs him and, consequently, a positive mark to the one who defends him. But, theoretically, there is a danger of the child forming the idea that the defending parent has a vested interest in establishing what a "baddy" the other parent is. This is not such a rare occurrence, and a regrettable consequence is that the child forms the idea that he can please this parent by recounting wrongs committed by the other. Some of my colleagues like to define this situation as "the child having power", and this matches the colloquial description of the child pitting one parent against the other. If this were an accurate picture, we should find a child gloating in triumph when the parents tear each other to pieces—but in fact these are some of the saddest children you can find. Of course, they have no conscious awareness of the extent to which their feelings are being ignored and abused by the parents. You may not agree with me and quote how such children become almost addicted to the reports of maltreatment at the hands of the other spouse, particularly when this is the parent seen for occasional visits. Yes, your objection appears to make sense, and the child's account may indeed mean "see what kind of person he/she is!", but it may also contain the question "can you understand what I went through?" And if you embark on a criticism of the other parent, you will be implicitly failing to take into account what the child felt and feels.

Whether the other spouse does or does not apologize should never be your concern. My argument may be clearer if we focus on a situation where the slight takes place in front of you. Father says to son in a harsh tone: "Why did you put my newspaper on the mantelpiece when I had left it by the TV?" The son, surprised, says "But I didn't do it, Daddy", at which the father lashes out with: "I'm sure you did! You never put things back where you found them!" As the son begins to crumple, the daughter says: "Sorry, Dad, but I was the one who took the paper." Perhaps the ideal father would now go over to the son, give him a kiss, and apologize, but the spouse in your question will probably simply snap some curt warning to the daughter not to do this again—saying nothing to the son.

The sequence must be familiar. The son will look at his father and, once convinced that no apology is to come, he will look to his mother. In films and television shows the mother will now turn to father and, quietly or loudly, rub in her long-held view: "Just like you, isn't it! You are forever jumping at conclusions, and what do you care about who gets hurt? Pigs will fly the day you pluck up the decency to say 'sorry'!" Have you noticed how, at this point, the child sinks into his chair? Yes, sometimes that child is depicted as glowing with delight that someone has taken his side, but he must also be aware of the hateful look that his father throws at him, holding him responsible for, once again, getting him into trouble. Furthermore, I believe that sooner or later he will work out that the mother has used this as another chance to lambaste her partner.

Suppose, at the point where the child looks at the mother, querying her response, she were to say to the boy: "Yes, sometimes you do tend to misplace things, but this time you were wrongly accused—I think you and Daddy have something to sort out on that one." Does this make a difference? If we are considering parents who live apart, the equivalent scenario would be that the boy is describing events that you have not witnessed. Nevertheless, I think the two types of comments would still apply. I believe that in the second answer you are acknowledging that the child was hurt unfairly, but you try to make him feel that he is able to fight his own battles, that he should learn to defend himself. Whether the father is essentially a brute or whether the child is fabricating a story or even if he is just getting things out of proportion, you can help him to define what belongs where. The first answer, to my mind, implies that you are more interested in creating or maintaining a particular image of the father than in protecting the child from him: after all, if the father is such a brute, why allow the child to be exposed to him? I remember meeting a woman who was left in her mother's custody after the parents' divorce. However bitterly she complained about how her father had treated her, the mother would passionately try to convince her that her father was really loving and well-intentioned. She eventually (that is, years later) turned this into a kind of joke, now being recounted to emphasize the argument that her mother totally lacked the capacity to discuss the daughter's feelings, holding on to an immovable view of her ex-husband. Actually, this particular configuration can sometimes be found in cases of children who have suffered abuse on the part of a parent (or other person, whether relative or stranger) and test out the other parent's capacity to take on board the child's feelings and experiences. When this parent responds by focusing on the other parent, there is a good chance that the child or adolescent will interpret this as a refusal to consider what he himself went through.

In summary, it is very difficult to deal with these triangular situations when your child turns to you for help over some trouble with the other parent or your present partner. There is such a tenuous line between the child feeling understood and supported, as against being undermined and dismissed! It takes careful exploring of the child's reactions to your comments, but the only advice I can give is for you to proffer more questions than conclusive statements. With luck, the child will guide you to what he finds the more helpful response.

I don't like my child's friends and feel they may be leading him astray: how should I react?

Whatever the child's age, you are not only fully entitled to make your feelings known, but you are also expected to do so. The challenge, however, is getting your child to accept your reasoning and follow your advice. Much depends on your child's age: the younger the child, the higher the chances that he will obey you—and it may also be easier to "get rid" of his friends at this age. The older your child gets, the more complex will be the child's feelings regarding all the thousands of precepts that you have considered important to build the person of the child you gave birth to. And it is these feelings—conscious and unconscious—that you have to win over. Sometimes it is worth "forgetting" that this is your child, who is supposed to listen to your words and take them to heart, and pretend that you are trying to convey something to a person whose language you cannot speak. This entails being completely aware of the message you want to impart, but then being prepared to express it in as many ways as may be necessary until your interlocutor grasps their meaning. Agreeing with you, obeying you, are your objectives, but they will only fall into place *after* the child has understood what you are trying to tell him.

The words you used ("leading him astray") seem obvious and straightforward enough, but they cover a wide and complex territory. By the time your child has friends, he will have absorbed a multitude of rules, behaviours, ways of speaking, and habits that will identify him as *your* child. Most of these are followed and put into practice in a totally spontaneous, unselfconscious way, and only occasionally will your child say or do something that can truly be identified as a definite departure from his usual behaviour. When this happens, your first impulse will certainly be to reprimand him and demand that he should stick to what you have always taught him to do or say. But it can be very difficult to establish whether he committed a naïve, unpremeditated slip or whether there was an element of deliberate intention that would deserve the label of defiance. When you believe that the latter is the case, you find yourself facing a dreadful quandary: do you ask him "why did you do that?" or, instead, "who taught you to do that?"

You will probably have distant memories of similar situations when you were the child in question. For you as a parent it is always tempting to blame someone else rather than holding your child fully responsible. But even when it turns out that he is copying what a friend said or did, it is possible that your child may be moved by feelings of loyalty, fear, and/or false pride to claim that he was the sole initiator of the behaviour in question. The clash can easily turn into a frustrating game where you can lose your temper if you are not careful. You happen to have a negative picture of your child's friend, and this can be accompanied by views you hold about his parents. In many such cases, your child may have quite a different view about his friend's character and/or family life. Your opposition can easily be understood, but it may be quite a challenge to unearth why your child has chosen that friend and what keeps the friendship going. Sometimes the friend has convinced your child that he has a ghastly family life and needs your child's support; at other times the friend is, instead, pressuring your child to submit to his demands. Either way, your child feels caught.

However absurd it may sound, I would invite you to think of the characteristics of the confidence trickster: I mean those fraudsters who manage to extort money from people whose gullibility makes us laugh at or pity them. But how do these fraudsters do it? They know what they want to obtain, and they have a sixth sense for figuring out what a particular person's Achilles' heel is. They will have a vast repertoire of techniques that they can resort to—and the result is that they eventually discover what that particular person is most likely to comply with. Politicians do this, and there is an amazing collection of other individuals and groups who put these techniques into practice. You find this in religious sects, but the same principles are applied in most marketing enterprises. The "guru" is now fashionable, to denote not only one's source of religious wisdom, but also the advisor contracted to increase a person's public acceptability. You are probably thinking of "brain-washing", but, however shocking, it may well be useful to bear such people in mind when you are trying to make sense of your child's deciding that the words of his friend are more valid than what you had always taught him.

The more common presentation of this problem is that your son may claim that he is being bullied into compliance. Whether he has yielded to threats or to seduction, I would say that the same structural principles of pressure are in operation as described above. At the end of the day, what-ever strategy your child's friend is adopting, the chances are that you cannot influence that other child. Of course, if the problem occurs at school, you should demand assistance from the staff. But, irrespective of whatever other efforts you employ in aiming to "eliminate" your child's friend, you should try very hard to understand your child's view of that noxious friend and then proceed to help him not to be a willing victim. If he learns your lesson, this should protect him from similar situations later on.

My children love to play with me, but eventually I get very bored: is it bad for them if I refuse to play any more?

A simple answer is to say "*No*": it is not bad for them if you refuse to play with them after having played together for a while. But, having said that, it might be useful to try to look into the implications of this "problem". From the children's point of view, it is fundamental to discover the needs and capaci-ties of each person they have to live with. You might put it the other way round and emphasize the children's need to recognize the impact they have on those around them. Either way, this is an example of the lessons that can lead to a happy togetherness. Once you reach "your limit" and you feel boredom begin to overwhelm you, the challenge is to find some way of stopping the particular play without making the children feel guilty or put down. You might suggest a different game if you wish to continue playing together. But if you want a breather, then a simple statement like "I would really like to do x-y-z now—will you play on your own for a while?" might do the trick.

What is likely to make your "problem" a more difficult challenge are the circumstances under which it arises. If there are other people at home, it is much easier to move aside and let someone else take care of the children. If, however, you happen to be the only adult available, you are bound to experience a wider range of conscious and unconscious emotions that influence your experience of playing with the children. To give you a simple example: your wife has gone out and left you in charge of the children; you play with them, and, gradually, you feel increasingly sleepy and bored. You remember the suggestion above about getting the children to carry on playing with each other while you go off to do something else. But it suddenly occurs to you that your wife may arrive precisely when you are in the kitchen reading the newspaper—and you imagine she may take this as an indication of your low level of tolerance towards spending time with the children. There is a good chance that you will then force yourself to continue playing with the children, even if now you contend not only with boredom, but also with a hefty dose of resentment against your wife and against the children for exposing you to such a possible confrontation. You can multiply the difficulties in such a situation by considering the possibility that you are the type of father who spends most hours of the day at work. So when you are sitting down and playing with the children, they will know that these are exceptional hours (and who can guess how they react to this?), and you will also be feeling quite self-conscious, if not downright guilty, that you spend "so little time" with them. With this last configuration, you can see that both you and the children will be half expecting surprises to be sprung on you: little room for spontaneity and unselfconscious pleasure!

I believe that your question highlights one of the most difficult issues in parenting. We must assume that all parents want to care for their children and spend time together with them. However, like it or not, parents have other duties and commitments, and usually it is outsiders who will have "clear" interpretations for each parent's attitude to their children. Your in-laws may criticize your being a workaholic, much as your parents will urge you to keep up with your father's devotion to work/professional life. The truth is that only *you* will know the precise extent of your capacity to spend time with your children. Leaving aside for the moment those multiple factors that refer to your family position, your workload, your personal likes and dislikes, and so forth, gradually you will discover that your level of interest and tolerance varies enormously according to the children's ages. Furthermore, the unspeakable truth is that each parent experiences very subtle differences in his or her capacity to engage with each one of the children. At times this has to do with gender, most often it involves their ages, but on the whole the developing personality and interests of each child will definitely affect each parent's capacity to engage with them in play or conversation. You may be familiar with the psychoanalytic theories that postulate projections (of significant people in our earlier personal experiences) we make on our children. This means making conscious or unconscious links between a particular child and another person who was part of our earlier life. But folklore has always been aware of this—for example, when we give a child the name of a loved relative—and this remains a link that persists for the whole of the child's life. Nevertheless, we must still make room for those strictly personal inborn attributes that each child possesses that will impact on the world of our own favourite likes or dislikes.

In more practical terms, looking after your boy who wants to play for endless hours with his model cars or his Lego pieces and your daughter who wants to organize her dolls and animals in elaborate family scenarios is likely to pose a formidable challenge to your patience and your diplomatic abilities! And if you and they know that you have hours to spare . . . well, I would assume that the children will be struggling with the same sense of hope and uncertainty that you experience yourself.

I hope this clarifies what I believe are the difficulties that you experience in the situation you raised. However, I would like to focus on the child's side of the picture. As I mentioned above, whatever images the children have of you, it is important that they should have endless opportunities to check what is the real you. Long before Freud explained it and rendered it as a concept, it was well known that each person is involved in a continuous process of elaborating (comparing, challenging, analysing) the images they have of people around them. There is general agreement that our perception of people is influenced by our previous experiences with other people in our lives and by the particular mood with which we approach them. Young children are virtually continuously exposed to their parents and/or caretakers. Obviously they react to each interaction with these adults with some emotional experience. From the moment that their neurological and psychological development enables them to retain a memory trace after each such contact, we have to consider that the next meeting with each adult will be influenced by the affect produced by the previous encounter.

Different psychoanalytic theoreticians have constructed complex theories on the basis of these affects and memory traces, but at this point I only want to emphasize that gradually the child will learn the real influence that his feelings have on the behaviour of each parent. If the child idealizes a parent and discovers that, in fact, this parent imposes some painful frustration when they meet, there will presumably be disillusionment, resentment, and anger. If the child meets that parent again and this time to his surprise, they have a wonderful time together, there will be relief, pleasure, and gratification. Whatever psychological theory of development you choose to adopt, I believe that the child's one and only chance of reaching a mature, clear, let us say enduring image of that parent lies in that parent being able to behave spontaneously and consistently. Easier said than done! Parents have their own lives to deal with, and when it comes to their children, the sense of duty and the obligations following from so many years of life and endless experiences they went through as children and as adults make spontaneity a very difficult commodity!

At the end of the day, your children are stuck: for better or for worse, *you* are the father they have. Their good and bad experiences with you, with your spouse, and with all others around them will influence every single occasion when you invite them to sit on the floor and play. I believe they promptly experience a whirlpool of ideas, conscious and unconscious, about what this session will bring. Because they are children they will tend to interpret every single disappointment as being due to them—that is, as not your fault, but theirs. Perhaps I should clarify: I believe that this is the case because children cannot afford to experience a parent as being at fault, since they want to retain an image of them as "good" so that they can count on them for further meetings. When you reach that painful, inevitable moment when you "have had enough", it is enormously important to respect your feelings and grant yourself a break. Children will always sense when you have overstepped your limits, and they can feel guilty for pushing you too far. This means that it is kinder to them if, as I suggested above, you say, "Sorry, but I really have to stop for a bit! You carry on, and as soon as I finish x-y-z, I will come back to you". If you manage to say this without any trace of guilt or failure, I am sure the children will recognize that you have reached the point where you need a break. This is enormously important for them, since they will gradually build an image of what exactly they can count on you for—without having to struggle with feelings of anxiety as to whether they have hurt, bored, or offended you. And, whether you agree with me or not, I do sincerely believe that children are enormously respectful of the needs of their parents. The art of this game is to manage to stop or to impose limits without guilt—if there is guilt, there is trouble, because the child will sense this and tend to blame himself for having inflicted it on you.

I dislike my child: is this unnatural?

I guess this question gets the top prize for difficulty! Nevertheless, the brief answer is "yes".

I have found that English-speaking people tend to give very different meanings to a couple of words that some other languages will use interchangeably when talking colloquially. In English, no one will fail to use "like" when talking about their reaction to a person's characteristics, whether appearance, speech, or behaviour. But there will be loud protests if this word is interpreted as referring to the sentiment we call "love". Occasionally, therefore, one can be told: "I love him all right, but I can't make myself like him!" Is this relevant?

I think this distinction is very significant. Love is not really a rational emotion; it cannot be subject to a discussion of reasons for its presence or absence. When it is missing in a relationship that is not amenable to change, the result is conflict and pain. But liking is a sentiment that refers to more tangible factors: it is usually due to well-defined attributes, quite circumscribed characteristics.

If I am interpreting your question correctly, I would invite you to put under the microscope the *reasons* why you dislike your child. Of course, if you are saying "dislike" as a euphemism for not loving him, then this is a more delicate situation. Not that you have to give up on your child, but that the factors in operation are probably less easy to unravel. Therefore, the crucial first question here would be to ask if you know *why* you dislike your child. If you were to name some feature of his personality and of his way of being, we would need to discuss whether this is amenable to change and to what extent you can bring this change about. If, instead, you would say, for example, that his skin colour reminds you of the brief encounter that made you conceive him or, to go back some decades, his physical deformities remind you of the Thalidomide taken during pregnancy, or, still, that his appearance and manner remind you of a relative you absolutely hated— how do you change this?

I suspect that, in practice, you have to be honest with yourself and gauge the intensity of the dislike. If you found that it is a sentiment that you simply cannot live with, I would urge you to look for a psychotherapist or counsellor. In other words, if your sentiments are aroused by some feature of your child's behaviour that you can influence and change—wonderful, here is a task you should be able to tackle. If, instead, the cause for your feelings lies in yourself and you have not been able to change these, do consider obtaining professional help.

6

Needing help, seeking help

How will I know when I need outside help or my child does?

In a sense, the answer is so obvious that this might appear a strange question to ask! It is so simple to say: "You know you need outside help when you perceive a problem but you feel at a loss as to how to deal with it." And yet, in real life, this turns out to be one of the most difficult issues to deal with. I am sure you have found that, whatever your area of work, not many people actually feel able to admit openly that they have reached the limit of their resources. It is a well-known fact that we are, all of us, much better equipped to spot faults and shortcomings in other people than in ourselves! When we do acknowledge some problem we cannot overcome, it becomes very difficult to allow anyone else to know we have reached this point of—to put it plainly—helplessness.

Friends and teachers will lecture you on the importance of recognizing your limits, the immense strength to be gained from trusting those around you to be helpful in a moment of need, and so on. But, for better or for worse, most of us find it difficult to ignore that thorny issue of our self-esteem. It is always quite baffling to see someone (someone else, of course!) continuing to struggle with a problem they clearly cannot handle and, unreasonably or illogically, persisting in their lonely struggle, presumably in the interest of saving face.

However, when there is a child involved, this introduces a rather complex additional factor. In your ordinary life as a parent, things will carry on in their own smooth way until that moment when you react with unexpected emotion to a particular condition, behaviour, or utterance of your child. Strictly speaking, at that precise moment, you would be expected to scrutinize your emotions and reach some conclusion as to whether the child needs correcting or whether it is you who is "overreacting". Of course, this ideal seldom occurs in practice, but when that situation is repeated several times, you find yourself wanting to "do something about it". But how can you establish whether it is your child who needs extra help or whether it is you who feels at a loss, perhaps having got the situation out of all proportion? In all probability, from a parent's perspective, you want to educate your child to adopt those behaviours that are part of your family ethos. But if the child does not respond to your injunctions, the search for answers comes into play. Difficult! And the situation can appear even more difficult if you have older children who, unlike this child, had no trouble in "fitting in" with your expectations.

The first step ought to involve you checking whether the child displays that same behaviour towards your spouse. Simple? Sometimes, but not always. Of course, if both spouses share the same perception of the situation, then all is clear, and the next steps are considerably simpler than if the two disagree on the interpretation of the child's attitudes. Bringing up a child is infinitely easier when both parents are agreed on how to proceed. Somehow, in most families, there is a repeated to-and-fro in the parents' attitudes to their child: one of them will protest about something, the other will say that he or she is being overly strict and will, consequently, propose a more tolerant response to the child. It is, in fact, quite fascinating (to an outsider!) to observe the way that parents will repeatedly swap their views on the child's behaviour. But even if the parents cannot agree on a shared interpretation of some behaviour of the child, it is very important to try to embark on a joint discussion on how to tackle the particular problem. To repeat: do try to deal with your disagreement with your partner, concentrating on developing a co-ordinated, harmonious strategy in your approach towards the child. What is at stake is not "who is right", but the attempt to establish whether the child has a specific block, difficulty, disability—something that might be causing his "reluctance" to obey you: and this may require professional help. These problems can become very awkward, because the moment the child knows (or senses) that each of you has a different view of his behaviour, you will find that this can influence his "wrong attitudes". This is when you find the child being accused of trying to control the adults or, worse still, trying to split the parents by pitting them against each other. Personally, I believe that no child manages to cope with the sense of insecurity that follows from seeing his parents clashing with each other. Misbehaving, "producing" the clashes, can become an unconscious attempt to see himself as the one at fault, which allows him to sustain an idea that the parents are good. Sadly, unless some change is brought into these dynamics, gradually the child (unconsciously) builds an image of himself as someone who has that particular behaviour as an integral part of his make-up.

One example: a 7-year-old boy is considered hyperactive. His father is a fanatical believer in the power of diets and demands that the boy's food intake should be strictly controlled, in line with his stipulations. But it turns out that when the father is absent, the mother allows the boy to eat the forbidden foods, arguing that no child should be deprived of eating things he likes just because of the absurd beliefs of his father. Given such a picture, how do we decide who needs help? When such a family come to a child psychiatrist or child analyst, it is terribly easy to get caught up in the painful disagreement between the parents and lose sight of what kind of help the poor child requires for himself as an individual in his own right!

It happens that I was caught up in such a situation myself. My father, in spite of working long hours, was quite involved in my upbringing, and I have many memories of his style of disciplining and teaching me. But, to repeat an anecdote I recounted earlier in the book, I remember very vividly one of many occasions when he would argue with me for a while and then say to my mother: "See what *your* son has done!" This was his gambit to say that he was at a loss as to what else he could do, so it was up to my mother to take charge of the situation. But my reaction took him by surprise. "Why is it that usually you say 'my son', but as soon as I do something wrong, then you say I am my mother's son?" My recollection is that the tone of his voice allowed me to see an element of humour in his words. But I have a very vivid memory of the anxiety I experienced, something like a feeling of being disowned.

Suppose that my father had said: "Oh, well, I've had enough, I can't handle this!" and addressed my mother—"could you please take over here?" In this rendering, he would be acknowledging that he had reached his limit and was turning to someone else who could help him out. However, his actual words made me feel that he was implying a failure of mine that could not be blamed on him. But I cannot imagine either of my parents being able to guess or setting out to discover how I felt when I asked my question.

I feel sincere admiration for every parent who consults me, whether this is expressed as seeking help for him/herself or for the child. I believe that asking someone for help indicates a determination to achieve the best for oneself and for the child. I am not referring to humility or other similar religious or moral virtues, but to the capacity to recognize one's limitations and, instead of covering this up or wallowing in self-recrimination and guilt, to turn to another person who might throw some light on one's difficulties and, thereby, again enable one to function better.

Returning to your question, I would say that, in practice, it is best to make your life easier and begin by considering that *you* are the one who needs help. Not that you should immediately run off to see a specialist: turn to your spouse in the first instance. If he or she agrees with your view of events, you can then plan a joint strategy to try to steer your child into different behaviours. If, instead, your partner disagrees with you, try to find a friend or relation whom both of you can respect and trust, and discuss your views with this person. If you and your partner agree with your friend's advice and you can put it into practice, this will either solve the situation or show that the child needs to be involved in the investigative process. If this is the case, then it is best to consult a professional who specializes in helping children.

You will hear many stories about people consulting child experts, and you will be surprised by the variety of techniques employed in this work. Results do not depend on the technique used in the interviews but, rather, on the sensitivity of the professional involved. If you are not familiar with this field, it is best to consult friends who have seen such professionals and then visit the expert you believe you may be able to trust. The one point to remember is that you are seeking help, and, therefore, the vital element to consider is: does the professional establish a meaningful dialogue with all of you? Do you feel that what he or she says makes sense? If it does, proceed; but if it does not—seek someone else.

The fundamental decision the professional is expected to make is whether the child has some intrinsic difficulty that requires a proper diagnosis. To begin with, you cannot know whether your child *actually* has a problem in himself: quite often, difficulties with children result from the parents not interpreting correctly the child's behaviour, and such misunderstandings can be remedied reasonably easily. A good diagnostician will be able to tell you what exactly is wrong and how to proceed.

My child needs help, but I'm worried— what if he is "labelled"? What should I do? What else might prevent parents from being able to seek help?

This question raises a formidable number of problems. As a clinician, I have met such issues many times, and they have never failed to shock me. If you recognize that your child needs "further" help, surely this means that you do not believe you can help him yourself: once you have reached this point, what is the logic for the mental torture you refer to? There is no doubt that once you ask someone else for help, that person will, explicitly or implicitly, expect you to accept specific conditions. If you are paying for this help, there is no problem, since once you settle the fees, you are free to disregard whatever advice you obtain. The situation is infinitely more complex if you turn to friend or relatives, as they might feel hurt or not respected if you ignore their advice. And, equally delicate, if you turn to an official body, you may have difficulties in disengaging from the system. It is therefore understandable that a mother may hesitate over having to involve someone else in her wish to obtain help for her child.

Having acknowledged these difficulties, we still must consider other points in this problem. If your child has a high temperature, you won't hesitate to take him to the doctor, but if he presents a learning or behaviour problem, you may find yourself incapable of making the decision to ask a professional for help: but how come? If you answer that one cannot possibly expect a parent to cure an infection with his or her love, you are implying that you perceive your child's non-physical problem as a reflection on the quality and efficacy of your love. Not very logical, is it?

Turning to the question of labelling, it is definitely not so certain that your child will be labelled, but it is most probable that you will feel labelled. I strongly believe that acknowledging one's limitations is a weighty challenge, but to aim for omnipotence and universal competence is a naïve and regrettable ambition. No mother feels a failure for sending her child to school to learn to read and write, so why should she feel a failure if the child is found to have special educational needs? Of course this is upsetting and extremely painful, but it is still illogical, even if understandable, for the mother to feel she has failed in some way. Yes, the child will be recognized as having special needs, but no mother would deprive a child of wearing glasses if this would enable the child to see properly. Therefore, if is *always* right to risk labelling a child as needing help, provided this help is necessary and useful. It should not really make any difference whether the child needs special education or hearing aids.

The question of labelling tends to surface when the word "psychiatric" appears on the scene. I like to quote a car sticker I saw one day when visiting Florida: "*It's people getting at me that makes me paranoid!*" It is probably correct to fear that a psychiatric diagnosis may in the future have some impact on a health insurance or job application. This has always been a possibility, and it has become even more possible these days, when all kinds of data are stored in computers that share their information in ways that we are not even allowed to know. But once this is acknowledged, is it really a valid reason to justify depriving a child who needs psychiatric assistance from obtaining it? Every time a parent telephoned me to discuss a consultation and then mentioned "labelling" as a justification for why he or she was hesitant to bring the child to see me, I thought this pointed to conflicts the parent him/herself had over the question of seeing psychiatrists. And it always made me very angry that a child was being prevented from obtaining what might well be a helpful consultation.

What most often stops a parent from seeking help is not social prejudices, the fear that the child will be "labelled", but serious problems of parental self-doubt and self-confidence. If you have a person or agency that you trust, the whole problem should disappear. This does not mean that this particular person or institution will give your child the help he needs, but you will not feel so lost. If you are or feel completely isolated and you have no one to whom you can turn for help, this is a terrible situation in itself. You may try to disguise this sense of being unprotected, by quoting factors like "social prejudices" to explain your feeling helpless, but this is hardly convincing and definitely not very helpful to you.

Which brings up the question of other possible social reasons for failing to seek help. One stems from whatever prejudices or pressures exist within a particular community; the decisive factor here, though, is the parent(s)' capacity to consider these preconceptions objectively. A well-known example is that of parents who are Jehovah's Witnesses and will therefore not allow their child to have a blood transfusion. Any outsider would say that parents should put their child's needs above their religious beliefs—but this is still a formidable ethical problem, since in most cases the parents do feel entitled to follow the precepts of their faith.

To pick up the opposite end of this problem: often I have found myself wondering precisely why a particular patient had come to consult me. One such example involved a 10-year-old child of divorced parents. Other psychologists and psychiatrists had been seen in the past, and the child was now attending a highly sophisticated school that claimed to offer teaching tailored to the needs of each individual child. I told the mother that the child had severe social and learning difficulties and recommended a specialized assessment; I told her that this was likely to confirm my view that the child ought to have a different educational input. First I was told that the father was convinced that the child's educational difficulties resulted from food allergies that required a carefully monitored diet. As the child spent most of the time with the mother, it became very relevant to discover that she did not share this view and therefore allowed the child to break the father's injunctions. Furthermore, the mother disagreed with my assessment and decided to let matters proceed along the lines prevailing before consulting me. I might well have been wrong in my assessment, but if I was right, this child would not receive the help he required: the father did not believe in psychiatric problems, and the mother was quite ambivalent in her views of the child's needs. How can we, therefore, explain the reason for this child continually being exposed to professionals who were not given the required conditions to offer effective help to the child? The nearest I got to an explanation was that the mother was aware that there was something wrong with the child, but she could only accept the views of those professionals who could reassure her that there was nothing wrong with him. This reassured him, if only temporarily.

In other words, there are parents who cannot accept the idea that there could be anything wrong with their child. It is tempting to hypothesize that they feel guilty for the presence of any such problems and, therefore, are compelled to deny them. If teachers or friends report difficulties that should be looked into, they will blame the teachers or friends and look for another school or break off the relationship. Unreasonable? Certainly, but such families do exist.

My child needs help:
to whom should I turn? Family?
Church? School? Doctor? Psychiatrist?

Once you reach the point where you decide that you must get outside help for your child, it is most unlikely that you know what is the precise kind of help he needs. I would argue that this means you should feel able to turn to any person you trust for that person's opinion on what might be the child's problem. But this is precisely the hurdle that you raise in your question.

Whether correct or not, whatever idea you have about the kind of help that your child needs will influence the choice of person or agency you turn to. Because you cannot be sure that your choice is the correct one, this makes it terribly important that you should turn to a person or agency you trust. But, to state the obvious, you can only make this move if you do have such a person or institution whose probity you feel you can rely on. You might go to your uncle, father-in-law, doctor, church, or any other social institution, provided you trust them—and you must then hope that they will give you considered advice. If at all possible, you should keep your trust under review and constantly check whether the help offered is, in fact, effective. Blind faith is the danger you have to protect yourself from. It is not relevant to which of these agencies you entrust your child, provided you watch the results obtained: if your child is not progressing, you should obtain a second opinion and, therefore, consult another agency or professional.

Different communities do, of course, have different resources. What is the difference between turning to a school, church, medical or psychiatric facility: simple! Each one of these thinks within their own "language", their own framework of reference. If you suffer from chronic indigestion and consult a gastro-enterologist, you are bound to obtain totally different advice from what a naturopath or homoeopath will give you. If you have recurrent nightmares and seek help from a psychiatrist, there is no doubt that his or her views will be very different from those of your priest. At the point where you decide your child needs outside help, there is no way of predicting who will be the best source of the type of help he needs. Of course you have professionals who can make a correct assessment and, if necessary, point to the most effective person or agency that will provide the required help. Sadly, these are not found that easily. Conclusion? You must turn to someone you trust and whose opinion you respect. This is no guarantee that you will obtain the help your child needs, but it is still better than seeking an opinion from someone whose words you will doubt and mistrust.

When my child needs outside help or is in trouble, how do I deal with the professionals I will have to see?

It makes a difference whether it is your choice to seek a professional or whether you are seeing one following a request from a third party. If this meeting involves your child, you may find it difficult to imagine what the professional in front of you is thinking. If you initiated the contact, you will have a good idea of what prompted you to consult this professional; if it was, for example, the school that recommended the meeting, you can certainly imagine the two main possibilities that apply: either that you agree with the recommendation—and this virtually places you in the same category as the person who sought the meeting—or, if you do not agree with the school's view, you are bound to feel and act very defensively at the meeting.

What about the professional? Believe it or not, he (or she) also has a mind-set before you even walk into the room. Whatever his job, he also wonders why he has to see you and your child. If you requested the interview, he will assume that the main "contract" is between you and him: you have a need, he believes and hopes he can fulfil it, therefore he gives you his time and expertise, and you pay him his fee (whether directly or through state agencies). You can well understand that the mind-set will be very different if a school or some other agency has sent you there. He has to figure out (or he may already have been briefed about!) what the agency expects of him, but he has no way of guessing how you feel about seeing him. Of course, he will hope that you will cooperate with him, but experience will have taught him that many parents in that situation are formidably defensive, if not frankly hostile.

A very pragmatic psychoanalyst, Michael Balint, defined very concisely the job of a diagnostician (he was writing about doctors, but I believe this applies to any professional meeting a client to discover what is expected of him). The professional has not only to identify what the problem is that brings the patient to the consultation, but also to discover (a) who *presents* the problem, (b) who *has* the problem, and—the most difficult—(c) who can be helped. This is the sort of challenge that your doctor, psychologist, or social worker has to face when you and your child meet him. To give you a common example: sometimes a school will refer a child for an assessment, claiming the child needs help. The parents, however, claim that it is one of the teachers at the school who has a difficulty that leads him to clash with that child. It is possible that the assessor finds that the child himself does have a problem, but equally he could discover that the child has no particular problem. In the former case, he can proceed to offer the necessary help, but in the latter situation his hands may be tied.

Perhaps you could consider this the first point to remember when you approach your professional: see him as someone setting out to help you, and definitely as someone who can do no decent piece of work unless you help him to achieve it. All professionals know that no client *enjoys* seeing them: nobody seeks a professional unless they *have* to. Nevertheless, professionals still hope that this is not going to be rubbed into their faces. So, try to be pleasant and cooperative, whether this is a terribly expensive visit or you are attending under some statutory compulsion. If you find that the professional is cold, distant, unfriendly, or plainly hostile, do not allow this to throw you off-balance. You cannot guess whether this person has just received some bad news, or whether he hates his job, or whether his appearance is a kind of test to check the client's motivation. Just keep your cool, maintain a friendly and cooperative approach, and remember that if you lose control, this becomes something that can be used against you. If you show goodwill, you may even find the professional relaxing and showing you a friendlier attitude.

The next point is important, but perhaps not always practical. Still, do consider asking how much time has been allocated for your meeting. Some professionals may resent such a question, but most will appreciate your wish to know whether you can take your time with your story or whether you have to be brief. I imagine that, like most other people, you have little awareness of how much time is "enough", but you are bound to have an assumption of how much space you are given at an interview. In a very subtle way, this will affect the speed of your delivery and your choice of "what is most important". Few things are more frustrating than approaching a painful encounter, plucking up your courage to be candid and honest, only to find the person in front of you beginning to shift in his (or her) chair and looking at the clock. It is always a good strategy to ask the professional how you can help, what he would like you to talk about: once he asks you questions, this will give you an idea of what he is after. If, instead, you just plunge into a long list of complaints (as, for example, accusing the teacher who seems to clash with your child), you run the risk of being seen as someone who is not prepared to cooperate.

When does the meeting start? Ask friends of yours about their last visit to the doctor, and I suspect you will get as many answers as the number of people you ask! There are an amazing number of perceptions that will influence your attitude to any professional. The little label showing you which bell to ring, that scratch on the door panel, the state of the carpets, the secretary's desk and her smile (if it materializes . . .), the kind of chairs in the waiting-room, the magazines on display, the way in which the professional receives you and whether he tries to put you at your ease, and so on. If he comes to your house, you will notice how he rings the bell, the way he dresses, how he greets you, and so forth. You will find that by the time the professional formally greets you and "opens the meeting", you have already collected enough impressions to ensure your confidence in him or, conversely, to wish you could get up and leave!

It is important not to dismiss any of these impressions. You should take note of every single one, because they will influence you anyway. It is more useful to register them, identify the impression they make on you, and then put these views to the test: only then will you be able to trust your opinion of the professional. There is no doubt that you attend in search of competence and not elegance or opulence, but do remember this if you should feel put off by, for example, the shabbiness of the place. This will affect how you address the professional, and he is bound to react to your manner. The more aware you are of your initial impressions, the better the chances of you giving him "a fair chance" to show his competence, whatever care he takes over the appearance and style of his person and his environment.

There is a fair chance that the opening remarks of the professional will give you a clue as to what he is looking for: "What brings you here?" "What can I do for you?" "How can I help?" "You will know that Mrs Smith has asked me to see you." "I understand you have been having problems with Johnny at school: can you tell me about it?" "I know you have been expecting me, but let me introduce myself: I am ____." I do believe that each of these will produce a different set of reactions in you. Different people prefer different openings, and it is quite difficult to analyse the reason for each person's preferences. It does make a difference whether you are seeing someone who has been recommended to you or someone whose name and profession is all you know about him or her. But the reason that makes your attitude so important is that you also want the professional to form a positive image of the new client he has in front of him.

If you agree with me that first impressions can influence people and that opening remarks will produce an important reaction, what can you do about this? I think it is extremely important that you should have a very clear idea of what exactly you want to obtain from that meeting. Once this is clear in your mind, all you need is to employ whatever strategy you have built up to get your way in life. Just pretend you are meeting your parent, your spouse, your lover, your employer, your sibling—whatever! If your style is to act humble, there is no point is adopting a façade, a strategy you are not familiar with. If you tend to be seductive, just make sure you don't overdo it. If your style is to be confrontational, there is a chance the professional will respond to you with the same retaliation that you get from other people. If you tend to be business-like, monosyllabic: go ahead, though you might just throw in some explanation like "I will tell you the basics, but do ask me questions, if you like." Similarly, if you are usually long-winded and forever going off on tangents, be fair (to both of you!) and explain: "I will tell you, but do stop me if you feel I am going off the mark."

My point is that if you know what you want to get from the meeting, there is a reasonably good chance that you will be able to adapt to the professional's style. Accept that he can only be himself and that it is up to you to help him understand what you are after. If you have no clear idea of where you want to get, you will probably find yourself simply reacting to the professional's questions and comments. This very easily turns into what is usually called "becoming defensive", which I suspect is usually the result of your taking the professional's words as reflections of what he thinks of you—that is, you take it all personally. This may well be the case with some poorly trained professionals, but on the whole they will ask questions and make comments about your child and the problems being presented; they won't criticize you as a person. A good rule: if you find yourself hurt or attacked by a comment, it is best to put it back to the interviewer. For example: "I understood you to say that I am holding things back, that I am trying to deceive you—is this really what you meant?" If you can say this in a quiet, friendly way, there is a good chance that you will get, if not an apology, at least an explanation of his words.

I think the above will cover any kind of meeting with a professional, but if you are seeing someone as a consequence of your child getting into trouble at school, a couple of points might be added. If the school believes that your child has a learning and/or behaviour difficulty and has referred him for an assessment, there are two possibilities: either (a) you agree with the school, or (b) you think they are totally wrong. Do remember that for your child to continue attending that school, you will have to accept the referral. But you are fully entitled to voice your conviction to the professional you meet, though I would urge you to see him or her as someone who might even turn out to be your best helper. So, in case (a) you might say: "I want to tell you that I am really relieved and pleased that the school have asked for this assessment, as I had been wondering about Johnny's performance." As for case (b), say something like: "I decided to accept the school's demand and bring Johnny, even though I am not convinced that they are correct in their view. I do hope you will have a good look at him and help me understand what exactly is causing the problem." Note here that you are not specifying *who* has the problem!

A final possibility is that your child is getting into trouble within the community—perhaps with the law. I am sure that all your instincts will push you to spring to his defence. On the other hand, it could be that you have long been defeated by your child's behaviour and you quite welcome that an outsider finally takes notice of this and decides to get your child to behave in a more socially acceptable way! Either way, the best advice I can offer is that you try to listen to what grievances are being put to you: don't immediately leap to your child's defence. Yes, someone accused your child of some offence, but the official may well approach you with a suspicion that someone is accusing your child in order to protect someone else. It is worth trying to look at the official as someone who is prepared to listen to you: this may lead nowhere, but your meeting the official with a barrage of accusations will definitely weigh against you. Remember, though, that authorities in this country are trained to consider a person innocent until there is proof to the contrary.